Follow In
*H*is
Footprints

ALSO BY THE AUTHOR

Who Is This Jesus?

Follow In *His* Footprints

MICHAEL GREEN

OLIVER
NELSON

THOMAS NELSON PUBLISHERS
Nashville

Published in Nashville, Tennessee, by Thomas Nelson, Inc.

This edition is published by arrangement with Inter-Varsity Press, 38 De
Montfort Street, Leicester LE1 7GP, England. Originally published as
Critical Choices, © Michael Green 1995.

Unless otherwise indicated, Scripture quotations in this publication are
the author's own translations.

Scripture quotations noted NKJV are from THE NEW KING JAMES
VERSION. Copyright © 1979, 1980, 1982, Thomas Nelson, Inc.,
Publishers.

Library of Congress Cataloging-in-Publication Data

Green, Michael, 1930–
   [Critical choices]
   Follow in his footprints / Michael Green.
     p. cm.
   Originally published: Critical choices. Leicester, Eng. : InterVarsity
Press, 1995.
   ISBN 0-7852-7069-8
   1. Apologetics. I. Title.
BT1102.G735 1998
239—dc21   97-44690
                                                  CIP

Printed in the United States of America.

1 2 3 4 5 6 BVG 03 02 01 00 99 98

For Colette

*colleague, friend,
and constructive critic:
in
appreciation*

Contents

A Word to the Reader

NEARLY ALL OF US LIVE BUSY LIVES. WE ARE surrounded by innumerable choices, and there never seems enough time to sort them all out. As a result we tend to go through life paying attention to the immediate pressures upon us, but content to stack the critical issues away to be handled if and when there is time. This book is about those critical issues.

There is a powerful story told by Jorge Borges in *The Library of Babel.* He sees the universe as a gigantic library. At first you are thrilled as you grasp the keys that allow you entry to the library. You are thrilled as you move along row after row of books. There is no problem in the world that does not have a solution somewhere on those shelves. But before long you give up in despair. There is far too much to know, too many choices to be made. Life is not long enough. You feel you know more and more about less and less. You came in looking for truth, and you end up confused, disappointed, and, like the librarian in the story, hoping against hope that there will be on some shelf a book that makes sense of all the others, and better still, a man "analogous to God" as Borges puts it, who can explain it all. But the man in the story dies in despair because he never finds that book or meets the person who could make sense of it all.

That is what happens if we shut God out of our lives. There is a Book that makes sense of the whole library of life, and it is the world's best-seller. There is a man "analogous to God" who can explain it all, and we date our era by him. He is not hiding from us in the recesses of the library. He has come to meet us. That is what happened at the first Christmas. But we turn our backs on him, do we not? We keep out of his way because he sees right through us. It is uncomfortable. We want to do away with him. That is what happened on the first Good Friday. But we can't get rid of him. He comes to life again. That is what happened on the first Easter. Indeed, he longs to come into our lives, clean them up, and become the integrating force in our personalities and our society. That is what began on the first day of pentecost, and has been happening ever since.

Think of C. S. Lewis, who came to Christianity out of profound intellectual skepticism and became one of the most integrated and influential Christian men this century has produced. Think of Alexander Solzhenitsyn, who trod much the same road in a Soviet labor camp and held high the torch of truth, faith, and human values in the darkest hour of Marxist persecution. Think of John Polkinghorne, who resigned the chair of mathematical physics at Cambridge to become a clergyman, so captivated was he by this man "analogous to God" who brought meaning and purpose to both human life and the universe we inhabit. They all faced up to the really critical choices, and then they lived by their decisions. They were confident they had chosen correctly.

In the midst of a baffling plethora of choices for our own activities and lifestyle, there is a Book that makes sense of it all, and there is a man who can be our guide. I have found this to be both true and deeply fulfilling; that is why I have written *Follow In His Footprints*. But I want readers to make up their own minds. We never take anything on board based on someone else's say-so. Therefore you will not find in these pages a heavy treatise on Christian dogma. It deals with practical issues we all have to face: our identity, our human predicament, our delusions. It teases out the possibility that sci-fi with its fascination for extraterrestrial invaders has hit upon a clue of the utmost significance. It looks at our longing for freedom, our strains and stresses, our hunger for love and relationships, and wonders whether these areas of universal human experience point us to the Book and the man "analogous to God" who can make sense of it all. If so, then the most fundamental of all human characteristics must come into play. We must choose. And of all choices we shall ever make, this could be the most critical. Shall we, or shall we not, follow that man analogous to God?

MICHAEL GREEN

Footprints

THE BASIC ISSUE

THE CELEBRATED ASTRONOMER CARL SAGAN opened his television series *Cosmos* with the dogmatic claim, "The cosmos is all there is or ever was, or ever will be." But was he right?

Sagan himself was not so sure as he appeared. In his later writings he found himself moving toward the conviction that there must be some mysterious divine force behind the cosmos itself. Which of us has not been struck by the splendor of the Milky Way on a frosty night and marveled at its beauty and immensity? "I can see how it might be possible for a man to look upon the earth and be an atheist," said Abraham Lincoln, "but I cannot conceive how he can look up into the heavens and say there is no God."

The trouble is that God is very much out of fashion. And that counts against him more than any arguments. It is not cool to believe.

There is a fascinating illustration of this point in the first of C. S. Lewis's *Screwtape Letters*. Screwtape, the chief devil, writes to Wormwood, his amateur associate, about the irrelevance of truth:

Your man has been accustomed ever since he was a boy to have a dozen incompatible philosophies dancing around in his head. He doesn't think of doctrines as true or false, but as outworn or contemporary, conventional or ruthless. Jargon, not argument, is your best ally in keeping him from the church. Don't waste time making him think materialism is true. Make him think it is strong, or stark, or courageous—that is the philosophy of the future. That's the sort of thing he cares about.

Screwtape goes on to observe that he once nearly lost a good atheist he had been working on for twenty years when he actually started to think and look at evidence. So he suggested to his patient, "That's much too important to tackle at the end of the morning," and filled his mind with thoughts of lunch.

Once he was in the street below, the battle was won. A newsboy was shouting the midday paper. A Number 73 bus was going past. And by the time he had crossed the road I had convinced him that what he needed was a healthy dose of real life to drive all that rubbish away.

Is it not like that with us? God does not seem a plausible hypothesis these days, so we do not bother to give the matter serious consideration. We squeeze all thought of these ultimate concerns from our minds under the tyranny of the urgent.

Maybe it would be a good idea to face the issue. Are we orphans in a land of no tomorrow? Are we merely a grown-up bunch of genes? Or is there more to the world and ourselves? "In the beginning God created the heavens and the earth," says the Bible in its opening sentence. That might just be true. If so, it has phenomenal consequences for all of us.

SAGAN OR THE BIBLE? WHICH SHALL IT BE? IS ANYONE THERE?

Well, if God exists, we might reasonably expect him to have left his footprints in the sands of our world. And please note that by "God" I do not mean the New Age idea of a god that is the cosmos and all that is in it, but no more. No, I mean a God with a capital G, the Creator, Sustainer, and goal of the whole cosmos—but by no means to be equated with it. The God who combines

transcendence (over and beyond our world) with imma-
nence (showing his hand within it). What footprints
might such a God be expected to leave?

Let's begin with a man who made few pretensions
to religious faith when he wrote *A Rumour of Angels*.
Peter Berger is a very open-minded and perceptive sociologist. He drew attention to a number of "signals of
transcendence" that we all acknowledge, but that are
very hard to explain if there is no God.

One is *order*. All societies have an instinct for order,
and it ties in with the order we see in the world around
us. "Human order in some way corresponds to an order
which transcends it . . . an order man can trust himself
and his destiny to," writes Berger. "Thus man's order-
ing propensity implies a transcendent order." If there is
order in the world, how did it get there?

Another is *play*. It suspends, for a moment, our serious "living towards death" as we experience again the
"deathlessness" of childhood. Play, he suggests, is a very
odd thing to find in a world that has no Creator and no
goal.

Hope is a third signal of transcendence. It is a universal part of human experience. It continues to the bitter end of our lives. It is like a silver thread, interwoven

with our experience at every point, but originating outside us.

A fourth strand of the transcendent in our experience is what Berger calls the argument from *damnation*. He thinks of situations where our humanity is so outraged by actions such as the Holocaust that we think no punishment, even death, is enough for the perpetrators. That is a very interesting phenomenon if death is the ultimate sanction. Where could the idea have come from?

Fifth, *humor*. What an astonishing thing to find in a world that has no personal Creator. Humor recognizes the imprisonment of the human spirit in the world and also, for a moment, liberates it. It gives a sense of proportion that makes our predicament for the moment tolerable.

Those indications that there is something or Someone beyond could be expanded considerably. I don't propose to do that now. Instead I would like to ask a question. Just suppose for a moment that the vast majority of humankind across the world and down the ages is right, and there is a God, a supreme Source from which all else flows. Go farther and imagine yourself God. After all, if the actress and author Shirley MacLaine could do that, why not you? What would you do if you wanted to reach out to the human beings you had made in your own likeness, but who did not want to know you?

Footprints in the Sand?

You might start by creating a marvelous *world,* a world that shouted out the love and skill and power of the Creator. Well, perhaps God has done just that.

Then you might create *people* who are capable of responding to love. People with the dangerous gift of free will, able either to respond to you or to reject you. They would have that almost divine capacity for self-determination and free choice. Well, maybe God took the risk and did that too.

You could then go on to instill in the hearts of these people *values* that spoke of God. Values like beauty, goodness, harmony, creativity, speech, truth, love. Of course, you could not force it on them. Free agents, they could choose the opposite—and often do. But wherever they are found, these qualities would point to the Giver, the One who is unutterable beauty, supreme goodness, total harmony, unceasing creativity. They would be the imprint of the God who leaves his footsteps in the sand of our lives. Perhaps God has done that.

You might like the idea of building in a *conscience* that would alert your creatures to right and wrong. A conscience that would approve when they chose the right way and would prod them and warn them when they went astray from your will that was their highest good. A conscience that would persevere however much they tried to stifle it. Could God have done that too?

You could after that instill a *God-shaped blank* in their lives, a hole that nothing else could fill apart from the living God himself. A space that cried out for satisfaction and fulfillment however much rubbish they crowd into it. A space that would elicit from them the cry that came to Augustine's lips centuries ago, "O God, you have made us for yourself, and our hearts are restless until they find their rest in you." Maybe God has done that too.

You might then show your hand in the course of *history*. You might ensure that the arrogance of nations and civilizations led inevitably to corruption and fall. You might concentrate on one man, one family, one tribe, one nation that would trust you and obey you, and that in time you could train to receive and perhaps even follow your directions. They might have to go through blood and captivity as they learned those lessons, but because the stakes were high, you would persevere with them and take great pains over them. So much would depend on their understanding and their lifestyle if you were going to be able to reach out through them to a whole lost world that was out of touch with you. Did not God do precisely that, with the people of Israel?

Finally, just conceivably, you might *come in person* to their world. You would have to come as one of them, for if you disclosed yourself in all your radiant beauty, they would be blinded by the sight. You would need to come softly and in disguise. You would need to learn their language so perfectly, without the trace of a foreign accent, that you could easily be mistaken for a native. It would be very costly. You would have to love them an awful lot if you were going to shrink yourself down to their level. It would be rather like one of us becoming a rat or a slug in order to communicate effectively with such lowly creatures. It would be an almost unthinkable sacrifice. But what if God did that too?

Reflect on one of the oldest bits of the New Testament, Philippians 2:6–11. It is from Paul's letter to a young church in Greece, and it is both emphatic and excited about the fantastic stoop we are contemplating:

Jesus Christ shared the very nature of God. But he did not consider equality with God something to be held on to. He made himself nothing. He assumed the very nature of a servant. He became one of us. And as he shared our human nature he humbled himself, and became obedient to death—even death on a cross. That is why God exalted him to the highest place in the universe, and gave him the name that is above every name, that at the name of Jesus every knee should bow, and every tongue confess that Jesus Christ is Lord, to the glory of God the Father.

Are we alone in the universe? Or are there footsteps in the sand, leading gently to the One who made those imprints and lived among us, died among us? We have the privilege of making up our minds about where the evidence points. We are free agents. We all have to exercise faith—the atheist's faith that there is no God, or the believer's faith that there is. It is faith either way. So how does it strike you? Was Carl Sagan right when he claimed that the cosmos was all there ever was or is or ever will be? Or had he missed out on the footprints?

Read on—for further footprints!

Identity

IN THE MUSEUM OF FINE ARTS AT BOSTON, Massachusetts, there is a remarkable canvas. It was painted by Paul Gauguin, and it poses three of the most penetrating questions it is possible to ask: Where do we come from? What are we? Where are we going?* Needless to say the painter does not offer us any solutions, and neither does anyone else these days. We are too much into our creature comforts and information highways to ask basic questions like that. Even the philosophers have for the most part given up: they have long tended to confine their inquiries to linguistic analysis. It is too threatening to face up to the really big questions such as these. Plato spent a lot of time examining the good life and the nature of justice. Aristotle went to town on ethics.

---

*Its full title is *D'où venons-nous? Que sommes-nous? Où allons-nous?* (1897).

But not the likes of you and me. Life is too short—and often too painful—for all that stuff.

Nevertheless the big questions do haunt all of us sometimes, maybe when we lie awake at night. They are questions to which atheism has no answer. And they will not go away. A fourteen-year-old put it like this:

> Why am I here? What have I done? Why was I born? Who cares about me? I am me. I must suffer because I am me. Why do we live? For love, for happiness? Why should I not commit suicide? I hate this world. I hate my parents and my home—though why, I do not know. I searched for truth, but I only found uncertainty. I was thwarted in my search for love. Where can I find happiness? I do not know. Perhaps I shall never know.

Dietrich Bonhoeffer, celebrated professor and patriot, had similar heart searchings as he lay in a Nazi prison before his execution for plotting Hitler's assassination: "Who am I? This or the other? Am I one person today and another tomorrow? Am I both at once? They mock me, these lonely questions of mine." But because he was a Christian, he could dare to end his reflections: "Whatever I am, you know, God, that I am yours."

More recently Bernard Levin, the journalist, asked poignantly,

> To put it bluntly, have I time to discover why I was born before I die? . . . I have not managed to answer that question yet, and however many years I have before me they are certainly not as many as there are behind. There is an obvious danger in leaving it too late. . . . Why do I have to know why I was born? Because, of course, I am unable to believe it was an accident, and if it wasn't one, it must have a meaning.

That problem of personal identity is both pressing and perplexing these days. There is biological engineering. There is massive manipulation through advertising. There is the pressure of fashion, the peer group, the unions, and the management. Not to mention the government and the job market. The sophistication of the computer age means that the banks, the police, the insurers all have a great deal of knowledge about me, so much so that there is a crying need for fresh laws to safeguard privacy. But in the midst of all this, who am I?

Am I just a number? That is what the prisoners in Auschwitz were. That is what I am to British Telecom.

Michael Green does not exist as far as they are concerned. But number EM 1524 4886 Q 072 GY does!

Am I just a combination of chemicals in suspension? Totally determined by the matter of which I am composed? That is what behaviorist philosophers want me to believe. I have just one problem with that. Who is the "I" who has made this shattering discovery? And what is the force of the argument that I am totally determined? Is it supposed to have a truth value? How come? For it, too, is totally determined by the molecules of the brain that makes the claim! All determinist arguments, which trash human dignity, are actually self-defeating. We are supposed to agree with them because they are put forward as true. But on determinist grounds there is no truth: I accept the argument or reject it according to the disposition of my mental molecules. And they are all predetermined! No, that will not do as an explanation of who I am.

Am I simply worthless? A lot of people feel that way today. Great numbers have been abused in childhood. Even more have never known what it is to be truly loved without strings attached. Almost half the marriages in the West today end in divorce, and recent research has revealed the obvious—that it is the children who suffer in a multitude of ways, but most of all in a sense of worthlessness. Nobody cares about me. It wouldn't matter if I died—and that is why an increasing number of under-twenty-fives, especially males, contemplate suicide, and many carry it out. After all, my parents don't want me. My girlfriend or boyfriend drops me. There are no jobs to be had, although I have had a good education. And if I am lucky enough to get a job, it will probably not match my education. For the first time in generations young adults today can expect to be much worse off than their parents. Anyhow, computers are replacing people all the time. So I don't matter. Our instincts tell us this is false, but circumstances conspire to persuade us it is true. Hence the confusion, anger, and despair so common today among the young.

Or am I wonderful? There are the optimists who say the world is getting better all the time, and that we had better learn to play the role of God. You have to live a sheltered life to believe that these days. Alex Comfort predicted that in a hundred years a world population of fifteen billion would each have three homes, two cars, and (rather oddly) one submarine, *given reasonable behavior*! Ah, there's the rub. We do not seem to be capable of reasonable behavior. There is a perverse twist in human nature. The world is not a better place: it is a wicked place. What generation has seen genocide like Bosnia or the Sudan? What century has witnessed such terror-ism, such slaughter of the unborn, such inner-city decay, such famine, such crime? No, I am not so wonderful. Neither are you!

QUESTIONS OF GENDER

The whole thing is made much more complex in this postmodern age. What does it mean to be a male or a female today? The gender confusion is immense. It comes over brilliantly in a film that unexpectedly turned into a major hit: *The Crying Game*. Here the female lead turns out to be a man, just as the relationship between her and the terrorist antihero gets sexual. But loyalty and tenderness remain, despite his prison sentence. It is a fascinating expression of the current confusion of male and female roles in society. Naturally this leads to widespread sexual experimentation, understandable but often full of pain and frustration. The perplexity and the anger of what has become known as Generation X run deep.

It is becoming rather less opaque for women than for men these days. There is still the injustice of work and pay inequality. There is still the glass ceiling above which it is highly unusual for a woman to rise. There is still the effect of the broken home and the shattered trust, in which so many were reared. Women are increasingly to be found succeeding in the workplace while their menfolk, who cannot get jobs, stay home and look after the kids. Writer Shirley Conran was not far from the mark with her "ideal" of *Superwoman*. But they face the agony of tension between career and home. They spend years earning degrees and doing professional training. It seems absurd to stop and give it all up. But it seems just as absurd to have a child and then leave him or her for someone else to raise. Despite the massive advance of the women's movement in the last half century the haunting question remains, "How am I best to deploy my life? Who on earth am I?"

Currently it is even more difficult for men. The Swinging Sixties changed women, but the Nurturing Nineties are changing men. The young men of this generation are the first to be raised on an equal basis with women. They are expected to be sensitive as well as manly, to cook as well as play sports, to bathe the kids and spend time caring for them, and not leave it all to their spouses. They are to be strong yet totally rid of male aggression and the overbearing arrogance that have, alas, been so common down countless centuries. And the change is all supposed to happen now, in one generation—a generation, moreover, when the woman may

prove to be the better breadwinner as well as homemaker.

Rosalind Miles in the *Independent* newspaper poses
the male dilemma well:

Over the past twenty years, feminism has been redraw-
ing the maps, rewriting the rules and redefining the
meaning of things unquestioned for thousands of years.
But we have hardly given a thought to the men. . . . And
many men are left feeling like lost boys in this post-
patriarchal world where their prerogatives and perks
have been blown away.

Where does the male fit in? Well may he ask, "Who
am I?"

That is precisely the question actor and writer Dirk
Bogarde faced as his career took off: "I rather liked it
all. There was one wavering doubt, however, just one.
Who the hell was I? There was a vast vacuum, and in
spite of a house, car, all my family and possessions, I
belonged nowhere."

QUESTIONS OF SCRIPTURE

What does the Bible say to all this? What does it say
about who I am and what I am worth? It gives an

alternative viewpoint. It offers a perspective of breath-taking wonder, surpassing all our wildest dreams. Something people long for but dare not imagine possible. As we saw in the previous chapter, it is evident in a man like Carl Sagan. He started out as a complete material-ist, but he radically changed his tune. In his book *Contact* he ended up with friendly extraterrestrials who come to earth to give us life, meaning, and relationship—a manifest substitute for God.

Yes, there is a hunger in our hearts for relationship, for being loved, for significance. And the Bible says, in effect, "That's not surprising. God the great Lover instilled those longings in your heart." In the first few chapters of Genesis we discover who we are. The picture is painted in bold, clear colors. And this is what it says.

If you want to know who you are, you have to start at the beginning. That means starting with God, the liv-ing, personal Source of all there is. And by the way, this is where the Christian teaching about God as Trinity is so crucial. The ultimate Source we call God is the arche-type not just of the one but of the many, not just the male but the female. Unity and diversity both find their origin in him. And when the Bible tells us that God is love, it means that his very nature expresses mutual self-giving, the benchmark of authentic love. He is both lover and beloved, and his love has overflowed in creativity—as love does. He has created this world of ours in love. He wanted to have beings outside himself on whom he could lavish his love. And so he brought humankind into being. That is why every one of us is special. Every one of us is valuable. There is nobody else in the whole wide world like you. You are unique.

God made you to share a common life with the animal world, but also capable of sharing life with him (Gen. 2:7).

He made you as the crown of the creative process, to be one of God's agents in exercising a benevolent control over the world, of which humankind is meant to be the responsible steward before God, not the rapacious capitalist. Authentic Christianity is inescapably green, though it has been disastrously slow to obey the calling of divine steward of our world.

God made us in his own image, and that image is best displayed in men and women together: a relationship based not on competition but on complementarity.

God loves us, amazing though that may sound. So much so that he is represented as setting humankind in a garden. Alas, we fouled it up, just as we are fouling up the world today. He loves us so much that he wants to share our lives with us and walk with us in the garden in the cool of the day (Gen. 3:8). But that is too threatening. We hide away from such divine intimacy. We rebel. We are not prepared to do the one thing he asks of us (Gen. 2:16–17). We turn our backs on him. We don't want to know. And shame enters in. Guilt and alienation enter in. Suspicion and mutual blame split the man from the woman. One of their children kills the other. The family becomes a battlefield. And God becomes the supreme threat, not the supreme lover. But lover he remains. He loves the man and the woman so much that he comes to seek them out when they are so keen to keep out of his way. Could anything be more contemporary? He has to judge them, in all justice; but then he makes skins to cover their shame, in all love. This timeless Genesis story shows us how much he loves the human race, so much that he finds a way back home for us even though we have blown it all comprehensively.

That is the God I know and love and worship. Indeed, only such a God is worthy of worship. His love, his splendor, and his incredible humility bring me to my knees. In the light of that origin, that price tag, that possibility of relationship and return, then I know who I am, where I came from, and where I am going. I do not come from plankton soup, subsist for a few years as a gene carrier, and then go out like a candle. No, I came from God. For years I turned my back on him and argued he didn't exist. But I have elected to turn back to God from my alienation and despair. I have found his loving arms the most dependable in all the world. I live this life in company with him. And at the end of the day my destiny is not just extinction but lasting companionship with him. If I risk all and commit myself to that worldview rather than the materialist and atheist one, it makes a profound difference to how I live.

QUESTIONS OF RELEVANCE

It makes a difference to how I look at *race*. Different races are not superior to one another, but complementary. Not enemies, but partners. Different, but coming from the same heavenly Parent, and therefore special and worthy of the greatest respect.

It makes a difference to how I look at *ecology*. This world is not to be raped, but to be tended. It is not ours, but God's. We need therefore to handle it responsibly and reverently, not just for the sake of generations to come, but quite literally for God's sake. Christians need to be in the forefront of the work of conservation. We need to campaign for higher prices to the consumer for things like coffee and fruit so that cash crop producers can earn a living wage and there is no need for impoverished native tribes to hack down the remains of the Amazon jungle for homesteads. I need to exercise and advocate personal restraint in the use of refrigeration, aerosols, and nonbiodegradable plastics that wreck the ozone layer with CFCs. Our ecosystem is delicately balanced. We are in imminent danger of destroying it and reducing our world to a wilderness within a generation. Ecology should be a major concern for any Christian who takes his or her faith seriously.

It makes a difference to how I treat *aged and infirm persons*, those whom society no longer considers useful. From a Christian perspective their value derives not from their health and strength, their capacity as producers, their usefulness to the community. No, it springs from the fact that they are designed to be sons and daughters of the Almighty. Their value is intrinsic to who they are, not acquired from what they do. That same respect must extend to the unborn. I cannot just liquidate them for my own convenience. Their lives, like my life, are God given, made in his image, special.

It makes a difference to my *sexual behavior*. As a Christian, I will see sex not as a plaything but as a sacrament

of self-giving in love between two married people who
intend it to be for life. Terribly unfashionable, I know.
But I am convinced it is the ideal. So, after years of advo-
cating the opposite, are the sexologists Masters and John-
son! It is, after all, profoundly human. What could be
more dehumanizing, more exploitative, than for me to
stay with my partner just while she is young, lively, and
sexy—and then to jettison her for a more up-to-date
model when she becomes obsolete? Yet that is what the
Brave New World of today regards as normal. It is not
normal. It is sick. I see the other sex not as *something* to
be taken advantage of, raped, and violated, but as *someone* to whom I can give myself in tenderness and intimacy for keeps. In our hearts we all long for love like
this. The trouble is, it is so difficult. That is where God's
help comes in—but more of that later.

It makes a difference to my *self-esteem*. I am not just
the student or the producer, the homemaker or the
number on a computer. I am me, the special, unrepeat-
able creature God himself has fashioned. The psalmist
knew this well:

You formed my inward parts;
You covered me in my mother's womb.

I will praise You, for I am fearfully and wonderfully
   made;
Marvelous are Your works,
And that my soul knows very well.
My frame was not hidden from You,
When I was made in secret. . . .
Your eyes saw my substance, being yet unformed.
And in Your book they all were written,
The days fashioned for me,
When as yet there were none of them.
How precious also are Your thoughts to me, O God!
How great is the sum of them!
If I should count them, they would be more in number
   than the sand;
When I awake, I am still with You. (Ps. 139:13–18 NKJV)

So I am not merely a load of chemicals in solution,
a bunch of grown-up genes. I am a child of God. I can
stand tall. I am not junk, readily disposable, essentially
irrelevant. No, I am a child of the Almighty. I have my
very own fingerprints and DNA, different from anyone
else in the whole world. I am valuable to the Source of
all life. So valuable that God himself bothered to create
me and sustains me moment by moment. What a mix-
ture of awe and confidence that instills!

And of course it makes a difference to how I look at *death*. No longer is it the ultimate dread. No longer the merciless tyrant that mows us all down with pitiless impartiality. It is not the end, but it is the end of the beginning. If I am linked with the God who loves me and will never do away with what is precious to him, then death is like a doorway into an inner room in God's house where I already live as an adopted prince or princess. Death is indeed terrible, but it will not rob me of that standing. Rather, it will bring me into closer relationship with God. Jesus was very strong on that assurance, and he gave good evidence that his word was to be trusted. But that, too, must wait for another chapter.

QUESTIONS

It makes a great deal of difference to how we decide on this great enigma of personal identity. Woody Allen hit the nail on the head when he said, "There will be no solution to the suffering of mankind until we reach some understanding of who we are, what the purpose of creation was, what happens after death. Until those questions are resolved, we are caught."

Think hard before you decide. Look East where reincarnation is the rage. Are you condemned to an endless recycling program until eventually the sentient "you" is extinguished and you are reunited with the universal One, with all distinctives, all consciousness, all identity liquidated? That is one answer to the question of personal identity. Has it anything to commend it?

Alternatively you can go with modern materialistic pessimism. You can follow the despair of a painter like Francis Bacon: "Man now realizes that he's an accident, that he is a completely futile being, and that he has to play out the game without reason." Rage at the situation, if you wish, like Dylan Thomas:

> Do not go gentle into that good night,
> Old age should burn and rage at close of day;
> Rage, rage against the dying of the light.

Rage by all means. It will make not one jot of difference to the outcome. But it will make a lot of difference to your sense of self-identity and worth.

The other option is the Christian perspective. Created by God, you are very precious to him. Precious because he made you. Precious because he thought you worth dying for. Precious because he affirms you and is willing to acquit you and incorporate you into his family. Precious because he is keen and able to share your daily life with you. Precious because he will employ you in his service. Precious because at the end of the day he will welcome you home. That is a marvelous understanding of personal identity. But is it true? There need to be good reasons if we are to accept it in a modern world that looks so bleak and meaningless. There *are* good reasons. Read on!

3

Aloneness

I AM CALLING THIS CHAPTER "ALONENESS" RATHER
than loneliness because what I am talking about is true
of busy people, popular people, successful people, and
not just those who are psychologically oriented toward
solitude. It is true of the fabulously successful. The singer
Michael Jackson, returning from a $70 million tour in
the East, went on record as saying, "I believe I am one
of the loneliest people in the world." And a Nobel Prize
winner for literature expressed himself like this:

> We fussed around talking trivialities. I wondered what
> the hell I was doing there, and felt out of contact with
> everything around me. Not a new feeling, but recurring
> more often. The two levels of living were growing fur-
> ther apart. The day to day superficial level had lost all
> meaning, and underneath where there should have been

rock had opened up a void of shriveling loneliness. It was getting worse. The present was bad enough: the future was an abyss. Only work brought my splintering self any sort of wholeness.

The celebrated painter Annigoni was once asked for what picture he would most like to be remembered. *Solitude* was his reply. He painted no less than twelve canvases about it. He said, "The whole conviction of my life rests upon the belief that loneliness, far from being a rare and curious phenomenon peculiar to myself and a few solitary men, is the central and inevitable fact of human existence."

This sense of aloneness is widely felt. Maybe that is why Harold Pinter, in 1995, revived his twenty-five-year-old play *Landscape* and put it on in London. There are just two characters, an elderly man and an elderly woman, apparently servants in a big house. They sit at a kitchen table throughout the play (forty minutes), and although they both talk, they do not communicate with each other at all. It's a classic statement of aloneness.

This sense of alienation is now so commonly felt that it is important to ask why. The answer is not hard to find. It has been superbly documented in Douglas Coupland's book *Generation X*. Generation X is a rather pejorative name in the United States for the baby busters or generation that followed the baby boomers of post-war years. We don't use the name so much in the United Kingdom, but we have the same phenomenon, and it is widespread. More than half the generation born since 1960 have come from broken homes. A majority of them have working mothers. They are the first generation of latchkey kids. A great many have been both physically and sexually abused, often by an older member of the family or a baby-sitter. They have watched tens of thousands of murders and sexual acts on TV. Sexual experimentation begins in the early teens if not before, and virginity is as much a stigma now as promiscuity used to be. Typically their parents both go out to work (if they can) in order to maintain a higher standard of living, but the children feel neglected. These parents give them the message that money and possessions are more important than family relationships. Home seems to many of them to be hell.

Bored with TV, they migrate to the street. In the gang they find the sense of belonging that they never had at home. If that leads to premature sex and drugs, to crime and violence, so what? Many of them have never known real love. They have never been exposed to reliability or undertaken much responsibility. It is every one for himself or herself. And raised by the me generation before them, who can be surprised if they think only of themselves? That's the only model they have seen. Who can be surprised if the kids sleep around? After all, that's what their parents do. Who can blame them for robbery and violence when they have been reared in a climate of financial corruption and domestic abuse? They have had to take care of themselves in order to survive. Nobody else seems to bother.

To be sure, a lot of pressure is exerted by home and school to go on to further education, yet when graduate unemployment is high nationally, there is every ground for cynicism. Many well-educated young people are either paid a pittance in some job for which they are overqualified, and from which they may readily be laid off, or they are unemployed.

In her remarkably perceptive book *A Generation Alone,* Janet Bernardi compares her fellow members of Generation X to random molecules bumping into other molecules. She goes on to make an important distinction between loneliness, which is a state of emptiness, and aloneness, where the life may be full of activities but lacks the support of family and friends. It encompasses, she says, a basic distrust of people and a fear of being hurt. It is a survival technique, and it comes across as independence. For a great number of people in their twenties today that is their overwhelming perception of life. Aloneness.

These young people are often disenchanted with institutions, and they hunger for relationships as the only thing that makes sense in our wasteland of a world. Some trust in just one special friend, and yet they fear that even that one friend may desert them and leave them with nothing but aloneness.

It will not do to blame this generation for the barbarism that is often apparent. They have been exposed to massive parental selfishness, to the worship of possessions, to the divorce of their parents, to the loss of the family as the norm. They have been subjected to abuse and neglect, to the lack of any moral guidance, and to spiritual starvation. Many of them have been through a poor educational system. They are condemned for the most part to a very bleak economic future and have been robbed of the hope that ought to belong to young people. Very few are optimistic about the future. They feel unwanted by their elders. They feel unloved. And if this is not the experience of every young person, all of them know that the majority in their circle come from such a background. Is it any wonder that many drop out? All that pressure on education and then few jobs at the end of it?

Even the boy-girl relationships are frequently unsatisfactory. Of course, they are the most important thing in life as young adults seek in members of the other (or the same) sex the love and stability they never had in their parents. But as all the popular songs recognize, ours is a society where we are free to abandon each other at a whim. Sex is a plaything to be used and discarded like a paper cup. And it hurts terribly to begin with until you get hardened to it and give up even hoping for the loving tenderness and stability that in your heart of hearts you long for. Young adults today have good reason to be distrustful of their peers and their elders alike. You're on your own!

As for the church, it is not worthy of serious consideration. Eighty-six percent of young adults have no link whatsoever with any form of organized religion. Part of the reason is that all organizations are suspect. After all, they have produced the mess into which the young have been born. The four bastions of bourgeois society, namely, the church, the law, Parliament, and royalty, have all shown themselves to be unreliable. The whole idea of organizations is alienating to the survivor mentality, to the person who has learned to trust only himself because all others have let him down.

But the disenchantment has deeper roots than that. The church is seen to belong to the previous generation and their parents, the golden oldies from whom the young have received so many hurts and whom they have learned to distrust. There seems to be massive hypocrisy in the church. Double standards abound. Sexual and financial irregularities are commonplace, even among leaders. Worst of all, religion is deadly dull. Keep well clear. Of course, if you want to be a wimp, stay involved with the church. But if you want to be real, to be yourself, keep clear.

TOWARD THE START OF TRUST

What has real Christianity to say to this profound hunger for relationship? Something that made an enormous appeal to me.

1. It tells me first and foremost that *I am loved*. Jesus went to town in his teaching to make that plain. He told us that God is like a woman who is heartbroken when she loses one of the coins belonging to the wedding band around her brow. She sweeps out every room of the house again and again until she finds that coin—and then throws a tremendous party to celebrate. We

are *that* precious to God! Or shifting from a domestic to an agrarian model, Jesus told us that we are like a sheep that has gotten lost on the mountainside. The shepherd does not say, "Oh, well, I've still got ninety-nine. Too bad that I've lost one." No. He turns out, whatever the weather, to search for that sheep until he finds it. I know no other faith in the world that pictures God in that way. I reckon such a God is worthy of my worship. Of course, it is up to you to make up your own mind. But to me it is mind-blowing that the God I have slighted and neglected should come to find me and restore me to a relationship I did not want—but was born to enjoy.

2. The Christian faith has another thing to tell me. That the estrangement so many of us feel from our parents' home is matched by a similar alienation from God, our ultimate home. That is why we find him so difficult even to mention—except as a swearword. We are out of touch. But the heart of the Christian good news is that God has thrown a pontoon bridge over that river of separation. The name of the bridge is Jesus. For Christianity is not really a religion. Nor is it an ideology. Nor is it a set of moral precepts. It is a *relationship*. A relationship with a person, Jesus. The One who claimed, and on good grounds, to bring the life of God into the human arena and show us, within the confines of a truly

human life, what God is like. That was part of it. But the other part is even more wonderful, if that is possible. He came to do a job. To get rid of the guilt that bugs us and sours our relationships with one another and him.

Our God cares for us so much that he came to deal with the guilt. It cost him execution, no less. It shows he has gone to the roots of our aloneness. He burdened himself with it. That is why you hear him crying out on the cross the ultimate shout of aloneness, quoting the psalms of David, "My God, my God, why have you forsaken me?" If you and I feel godforsaken, we can rest assured that God himself knows that feeling from the inside. You can trust a God like that, however much other people may have let you down—can you not?

3. But the Christian gospel reaches more deeply into our essential aloneness. What it offers us is this. Not a God who is so far above us that he seems miles away. Not even a model of how life ought to be lived—useful though that might be. But our God (who *is* miles above us and *did* come to be our example) offers to be our *constant companion*. That is the heart of Christian discipleship: friendship with a God who will never leave us or forsake us. The New Testament dares to assert that "God does not live in temples made with hands: your body is the temple of the Holy Spirit." It tells us to "be

content with such things as you have. For He Himself has said, 'I will never leave you nor forsake you.'" No wonder the writer continued exultantly:

> We may boldly say:
> "The LORD is my helper;
> I will not fear.
> What can man do to me?" (Heb. 13:5–6 NKJV)

That is staggering! The living God himself is prepared to come and share our very lives with us. What a friend! Think of your very best friends. There are a couple of snags about even them, are there not? In the first place they can't be with you all the time—only sometimes. And second, you have a horrible feeling that if they really knew what you are like deep inside, they might well drop you. Well, the Lord offers to be the friend who will never leave you or forsake you. He will never let you down and never give you up. Moreover, because of what he did to carry the load of "the bad thing" on the cross, you can really trust him when he promises that nothing in all creation will be able to separate you from his love. He is the One, the only One, who knows the worst about you and loves you just the same.

4. There is one other way in which God in his kindness offers to meet our aloneness. When we stop running away from him and come back and say, "Sorry," an amazing and irrevocable thing happens. It is a radical *change of status*. God adopts us into his family. We become sons and daughters in his family. We are adopted alongside Jesus Christ. Inevitably, then, we find ourselves brothers and sisters of others who have been welcomed into that relationship. You don't choose your brothers and sisters—and that holds for ordinary life and life in God's family as well. You are stuck with them! But the marvelous thing is this. God pours into our hearts a new bonding for others in the family. Indeed, John said that this new "love for sibling Christians" is one of the more sure marks that we really have come back to God and made a new beginning.

I can certainly confirm that from my own experience. I became a follower of Jesus Christ in my teens in the same summer as a boy whom I heartily disliked. When we came back for the next term, we found ourselves in the same Christian fellowship within the school. We regarded each other as warily as a couple of fighting cocks until we discovered, very speedily, that a new chemistry was at work. God had amazingly taken away our mutual hostility and replaced it with a real bonding that could only have come from God. It certainly did not come from us. That transformation is quite typical when people become followers of Jesus. I have seen badly damaged folks come to a new happiness, a fresh ability to trust once again, and a restored self-respect. Problems, of course, do not vanish, but God somehow wipes away the pains and disappointments, the abuse and the hurts, the sins and the failures of the past and gives us a completely new sheet.

As a matter of fact that is just what he does. The New Testament is full of it. It describes it not just as forgiveness but "justification": a full legal acquittal from all the accusations and garbage from the past. How is it possible? Because God himself has handled "the bad thing," and it doesn't need to be done twice. Read all about it in the New Testament. Try Paul's letter to the Romans, the first eight chapters; or if you want it in brief, start with Romans 5:1 or 8:1. Anyhow, what this profound slate-clearing does is this. It enables us to approach God with confidence as those whom God himself has acquitted—and "if God is for us, who can be against us? . . . It is God who justifies. Who is he who condemns?" (Rom. 8:31, 33–34 NKJV). Thus gradually, painfully gradually, confidence returns, love and trust begin to blossom again, and we find ourselves in a company of people who accept us. They do so for the very good reason that they, too, have been accepted unconditionally by God, and been given love without strings that is the most nourishing fare in the world.

Of course, there are lots of failings in the Christian community. Everyone knows that. New Christians are rather like abandoned houses that have just been purchased and need massive reconstruction. The Master Carpenter has made a start on it, but he hasn't finished with us yet. So do not be too surprised at failure and disappointment either in yourself or in the Christian community. The battle between what we were and what we become once Christ is allowed a hand is lifelong. But I believe you will find it abundantly true that the Christian family has a wonderful warmth to it, especially as you get together with a small group of Christian friends and learn to trust again . . . and love again . . . and hope again. You see, God is not just interested in individual restoration. He wants to replace aloneness with a new society, the Christian family, the church—call it what you will. I like to see it as God's counterculture. It is the Community of the Resurrection because it is companionship with the risen Jesus.

It takes trust to get started—but that trust is well grounded.

4

Story

THE REDISCOVERY OF STORY

It is fascinating that in this sophisticated age, dominated by technology, people should be turning back so eagerly to the story. Story is the genre of the most popular and long-running TV programs, such as *ER, Touched by an Angel,* and the rest. It is the story that sells the local paper. In recent times it is evident that quality newspapers are taking a leaf out of tabloids and going for stories about real people, their heroism, their shame, their fate. Why is it that the Narnia stories are constantly attractive to thousands of people who would never read C. S. Lewis's theological or literary writings? Because they are story. And story is one of the most timeless, attractive, and memorable ways of communicating anything.

But that is not the only reason why it is currently regaining such significance. We are living at one of the hinges of history. For two and a half centuries the developed world has been governed by the assumptions of the Enlightenment. Reason was king. This world was all there was. Science was the way to pierce its secrets. Technology was the way to appropriate its benefits. Truth was reduced to what could be measured or weighed. Debate was carried out on the principles of formal logic. Morals were deemed universal: based not on some supposed divine will, but on a calculation of what would serve the greatest good of the greatest number. Religion was privatized. The supernatural was discounted and miracles dismissed as impossible. Nothing was sacred. Rational doubt was the way to advance knowledge. God was banished from the marketplace of life to a sort of House of Lords where he could do no harm and exercise no power.

All that is changing. There is today in what we call our postmodern society a major change of direction. We are no longer persuaded that science is the arbiter of all advance. Within our lifetime it has opened up a whole Pandora's box of horrors. Brian Appleyard, writing in the *Independent* newspaper, points out: "In the mind of the public, science is no longer the virtuous guide to a better future, but a deeply ambiguous form of knowledge that offers as many threats as it does consolations." Science, of course, is neutral. It is what human beings do with its discoveries that can be horrific. Then again we are no longer so credulous about the rationality of the human race. We make most of our critical decisions in life on grounds other than cold reason! Jung and Freud have shown, in any case, that reason is far from king. Philosophy and history are both at a discount in many circles these days; they are part of the old structural basis on which the Establishment has exercised its dominance.

Why should the left side of the brain have been allowed ascendancy for so long? It is time for the right side to be heard. And so truth gives way to relativism. Dogma yields place to pluralism. Rationalism is seen to be the worship of a particularly barren idol. The reductionism of radical doubt robs life of color and meaning. And why banish the supernatural? Thus we have seen a tremendous burgeoning of the nonrational, the existential, the occult—particularly but not exclusively in New Age thinking. There is a new hunger for spirituality, a new concern to preserve the environment from destruction by capitalist greed, a new openness to the paranormal, a new sense of mystery, a new celebration of life, and a new moral and spiritual autonomy. Many see us as parts of a universal monad, which is nothing less than divine.

There are many darker sides to this new scenario, and it is hotly contested. But there can be no doubting the fact that we are living at a time of major cultural change. All the goalposts are mobile nowadays. And in the midst of this exhilarating, if confusing, scene we are rediscovering the story. It is the carrier of reality. It speaks to the whole of our human condition.

THE CHRISTIAN STORY

So be it. The Christian will have no objection to leaving the lists of rationalistic combat and reverting to the medium in which the gospel first fell on human ears. We, too, have a story to tell, and we may be pardoned for thinking it is the most marvelous story in the world. We are not embarrassed either by competition from other stories or by challenges on grounds of truth. We know this story is gripping thousands of new adherents worldwide every day, in developed and developing countries alike. It keeps spreading, in the heat of sub-Saharan Africa as well as in the frozen wastes of the Arctic. It appeals equally to men, women, and children, as a really good story should. It appeals to people of all faiths, and those of no faith. And like the very best of stories, it enables the hearer to identify with it and feel that the story is his or her story. It runs something like this.

In the beginning God created the heavens and the earth. That is where it all begins—all good stories need a clear beginning. This one is very clear. You can't go back behind God. He is the ultimate Source of all there is. A Source beyond ourselves and our habitat, a Source that is personal and yet transcends personality. This God is the origin of life. This God is the Sustainer of natural laws. This God is the moral Ruler of the universe and will be its Judge. This God is love. His very nature is generous self-giving. And our story is the account of his dealings with the human race.

There are two major obstacles to our having much knowledge of him. The first is our sheer humanity. We are small and strictly limited in our understanding and insight. How could we be expected to pierce the incognito of the Source, Sustainer, and goal of the universe? The second is even more serious. We are self-centered. Our lives are riddled with pride, greed, lust, aggression, jealousy, indifference to other people's suffering, and the like. God cannot be pleased with what he sees. Are you pleased with what you see around you, in society, in your friends, in your family, in yourself? If you are— and I take leave to doubt your honesty if so—pick up a Sunday paper or watch a news program. You will soon be persuaded of the fundamental fact that the story maintains: humanity is desperately flawed. It is dangerously diseased.

We cannot know God because he is beyond our puny minds. We cannot get through to him because his purity shrivels our endemic human wickedness. Our approach to him being thus excluded, the story tells us that he decided to approach us. All through history he has been reaching out to humankind. He called Abraham two thousand years B.C. to follow him in trust and obedience. Abraham did, and he became the pioneer of the people of faith. From him sprang the Jewish nation, and gradually that nation learned the holiness and judgment, the love and forgiveness, of the God who was calling them. They slowly learned to uphold the one true God against all the background of religious pluralism to which they were exposed. They learned to trust him through disaster and captivity. But he still remained to a large extent the unknown God. They were still aware of the aloneness that we addressed in the last chapter.

And so to what R. S. Thomas calls *The Coming*. He imagines God holding in his hand a small globe, drawing his Son's attention to it. The pain and anguish were all too apparent. On a bare hillside a bare tree held out its arms—and many people looked to it in hope. The Son watched them and said, "Let me go there."

That is what happened. Without abandoning his control over the universe, God came in the person of Jesus to share our situation. He was not dressed up as man: he was man. He was also God. Not all of God there is (he often spoke of his heavenly Father as greater than himself) but all of God we could take in. All of God that could be crammed into human flesh and blood. Do not misunderstand the story at this crucial point. It does not claim that God was exhaustively embodied in Jesus of Nazareth, but that Jesus gives us a true window into God, without distortion. It is rather like an iceberg. What we can see above the waves is only part of the whole iceberg, yet it is all of a piece with the part we cannot see. Jesus brought God out of the waves of unknowing. He brought God into focus and laid himself open to our scrutiny and assessment.

The Power of the Story

The story of Jesus is the most beautiful in all the world. No wonder one-third of humankind are moved by it. No wonder it has never been matched, let alone eclipsed. Read the Gospel of Luke through at a sitting if you want to grasp the power and the beauty of this story.

The teachings of Jesus, his loving actions, his healings, his miracles, his claims—all spring from what he is: both man as he ought to be and God as he is. That is what makes him totally unique. That is why Christians cannot agree to have this story put on the same shelf as other stories. All the others have varying degrees of truth in them, or they would never have gained any readers. But theirs is the appeal of the twilight. This story has the immediacy and power of the blazing sun. When the perfect story is told, the preparatory and the partial recede. From now on we do not have to make do with an unknown God: "In Christ the whole fullness of the Godhead dwells bodily" (Col. 2:9).

Why did Jesus, who shared God's nature and God's home, bother to make this great descent? Why did he steadfastly set his face toward that terrible cross, which has become a worldwide symbol of loving service and total self-sacrifice ever since? He did not go there just to set a great example of self-giving—though that was part of it, a part our hedonistic and selfish society could well take on board. He did not go to the cross just to show us how much God loved us, though it did demonstrate that conclusively. He went there to bring us back to God. He went there to fashion a bridge over the troubled waters of our alienation and self-centeredness. He came to do what the bulldozers have been doing—opening roads between the North and South of Ireland after men had at last begun to come to their senses and laid down their arms. He came to construct a road back to God out of the hostilities that have prevailed too long. He did it at phenomenal cost and in a perfectly astonishing way.

The point is this. Our human wickedness had cut us off from God. It had made an impenetrable barrier between the two parties. What Jesus did on the cross was to break through that barrier. He made a road back to God for people who admit they are in the wrong and are prepared to accept reinstatement as a free gift from the heart of a generous God. Why should he need to go to such extremes? we might ask. Simply because forgiveness is never cheap. Our failures and acts of rebellion hurt God. They outrage his holiness. If he was to remain the moral arbiter of the universe, he could not ignore them. But if he acted in judgment on them, as he fittingly might, there would be no hope for any of us. So he became one of us, and in our place bore the alienation, the judgment that was our due. That is how much he cares. There is no comparable story in all the world.

Lingering Doubts

But lingering doubts remain. Why should he have to die in order to restore relations between God and us? The answer takes us back almost to the very beginning—when human beings first rebelled against God. In the matchless story of the Garden of Eden you may recall that God had warned that death would inevitably follow disobedience: if humankind chose to reject God, he could do no other than confirm their choice. Had he not entrusted them with freedom? The devil persuaded them that this warning could safely be disregarded. They ate the forbidden fruit, and as we saw in a previous chapter, at once they shriveled and died spiritually. They lived on mentally, physically, and socially for their life span, but then the spiritual death that already prevailed in their lives was finalized by physical death.

It was the spiritual life that Jesus sought to restore for a fallen world. So he did not merely show his love and solidarity with us by sharing the most ghastly form of physical death, but he allowed himself to suffer the alienation, the damnation if you like, that our evil deeds deserved. He died our spiritual death so that he could with perfect justice offer us his spiritual life. He took our guilty place on Calvary so that we could share his place of perfect acceptance with God the Father. That is why his death was so important. It restored relations with God by absorbing our hostility and guilt that had conspired to cut us off. That's how much he loves us!

There's another issue, which arose almost as soon as the story came to be told. Why should he die on a cross of all places? Was that significant? Yes, the story is clear that it was. You see, the Old Testament, which was deeply written onto every Jewish heart, was clear on the point that anyone exposed to die on a stake must be resting under the curse of God. It was all there in Deuteronomy (21:23). So it was perfectly plain to all and sundry that when Jesus was exposed to die on a cross, he was suffering the curse, the righteous judgment, of God. How could this be? Everyone knew that he had lived a matchless life. The answer dawned on them rather fast, and it was this that gave the story such a universal appeal. He did indeed die under God's curse. But the curse he bore was ours.

Paul was very clear about this when he was recounting the story. He told us that all who rely on their good deeds to get them to God will rest under the curse of God's righteous judgment. Does not the Old Testament make it clear that everyone who does not obey all the commands of God in the Law of Moses merits that curse? And which of us could claim to be blameless before a holy God? Then Paul erupted with this triumphant explosion: "Christ has redeemed us from the curse of God's broken law by becoming a curse for us—for it is written, 'Cursed is everyone who hangs upon a tree'" (Gal. 3:13). So that is why the manner of his death mattered. It showed he had faced and personally absorbed our guilt that merited God's judgment. We can now with perfect propriety be welcomed back. What incredible love!

Part Two of the Story

But that is only half of the story. It goes on to relate how death proved unable to hold Jesus down. That, of course, seems totally incredible to us who have never witnessed a perfect life. We know only people in whom evil has gained a real foothold. We are all, without exception, flawed examples of what it means to be human. So when our friends die, that is it. Death has an awesome finality about it.

But we have no idea if the same would be true of someone who was perfect. There has been only one such person in the history of the world. And by all accounts he rose again from the grave in which he was buried. Ancient historians reckon that the resurrection of Jesus on the first Easter is one of the best-attested facts in all history. It was the start of the Christian movement: Christianity got off the ground only because Jesus rose from the dead. They maintained then, and they have maintained ever since, that he is alive and can be met and known by anyone who is prepared to fulfill the conditions. I am not for the moment asking you to believe this part of the story. I am simply asserting that the Resurrection lies at the heart of Christianity. Christians believe that *Jesus is alive*.

Implications of the Story

If we have come to believe the story, it makes a great deal of difference to our lives and outlook. It leads us to reverence this world as God's gift. It helps us to make sense of both the goodness and the evil in society and in ourselves. It gives us a new estimate of Jesus and constrains us to bow in worship before him. It exhilarates us with a sense of pardon and reinstatement—alienation banished, guilt removed. It gives a new angle on death. Death has had its claws clipped. Jesus told his followers that they would join him after death. And when he backed those words by actually rising from the grave, is it surprising that they were convinced? Faith in the afterlife began to strengthen Christians to face death unafraid and to wipe away some of the tears of Christian mourners.

But there are other implications in this story. It shows us that real Christianity is not just pie in the sky when you die. A lot of the pie is for now. For if God came to this world for us, it must be a rather special place. It means that the followers of Jesus must engage with modern society and use all their effort to make it a better place. True followers of Jesus do not write this world off and wait for the next. They try to get involved in the problems of the illiterate, the sick, the people of the inner city, the mentally disturbed. You will find them in business and in government, in the caring professions and in every walk of life where they can make a difference.

The social implications of the story are very far-reaching. The followers of Jesus attempt, in his strength, to give off an aroma of God's way of life in their relationships, service, and aspirations. They see themselves as forerunners of God's kingdom, the first installment of a future crop. So, for all the weakness of the church there is a strong strand of hope in authentic Christianity. The hope of exhibiting the love and self-sacrifice of Jesus here, and the hope of being with him hereafter. There is nothing selfish or individualistic, narrow-minded or earthbound, about Christianity. It is a total response to the great God who has totally given himself out of love for us. When that really gets to you, it makes big changes.

That is the outline of the story and its implications. It is still unfinished because all of us have the opportunity to become part of it. Each of us has to decide whether to believe the story. It is a totally new way of looking at life. It will affect everything we do—just as it would if we had spent all of life with sunglasses on and then suddenly removed them, or had only an old black-and-white TV and then suddenly acquired a color set. It changes everything. The story has that power to transform. So we need to be rather careful in assessing it. It might be true. If so, it is of incomparable value. It might not, in which case we will want not only to reject it but also to throw all our influence against it. We have to choose.

And that choice should be determined by evidence. Does the story hold up? Is it credible? This is a crucial question because the story claims to be history, indeed his story. It is good news about a unique historical person who was born less than a generation before the Gospels were written and was executed very publicly under the Roman prefect of Judea, Pontius Pilate. He claimed to embody God's self-disclosure to the human race and to rescue us from the consequences of our folly and rebellion. He backed that claim with his matchless teaching, his perfect life, and his well-attested resurrection.

Nowhere in all the world's religions is there anything remotely comparable to this story. It has, indeed, features in common with the nature worship underlying so many of the Eastern religions, based as it was on an annual cycle—the birth, maturity, death, and resurrection of the year in its four seasons. The ancient Orient had many variations on this theme of death and resurrection in the cults of Dionysus, Attis, Isis, Cybele, and Mithras. But with this story there was a fundamental difference. It was all attached to a historical person, a very special person, whom lots of the readers will have known personally. It is all about the Jesus of history. Remove him from the center of the story, and there is nothing of substance left. Many of the ideals can be found elsewhere. Much of the ritual is universal coinage. But once disprove the historicity of Jesus and the whole story collapses. So it should. For the claim is that these things happened, that God did come to us in the flesh of Jesus, that he did die for us on that cross, and that he is alive, risen from the dead and relevant to individuals and societies today. And that is a matter not of mythology or ideology but of history. How well founded is that claim? We will look into it in the next chapter.

5

Extraterrestrial

FEDERICO FELLINI, THE LATE CELEBRATED ITALIAN FILM director, had a depressing view of life. "Like many people," he wrote, "I have no religion. I am just sitting on a small boat, drifting with the tide. I just go on cutting, editing, shooting, looking at life, trying to make others see that today we stand naked and more defenseless than at any time in history. What I am waiting for I do not know—perhaps the Martians will come to save us."

I greatly admire the courage of an atheist like Fellini. He had no hope, but all the same he worked on in hope, with nothing better to sustain him than a fancied intervention from a planet where he knew perfectly well there is no such life. There is a rash of interventionist writings from the science fiction lobby these days, and it has an enormous following. Just think of the way the

Star Wars films, *Close Encounters,* and *ET* engaged the popular imagination. Think of the continuing grip of *Star Trek* on its Trekkies. Even as I write, the program that gains the highest ratings on BBC2 is *The X Files,* a drama investigating UFOs and the paranormal, while sci-fi authors crowd the bookshelves. Harmless imagination, to be sure. But it is also highly significant. Many thoughtful people like Fellini despair of the mess we have gotten the world into and are longing for a rescuer from outside, an extraterrestrial. But we know in our heart of hearts that it is a vain hope.

Curiously enough, the Christian faith is all about an extraterrestrial. Jesus Christ claimed to be just that: a rescuer from outside who can make a real difference to our lives, our society, and our world if we allow him to do so. We saw the essence of the story in the last chapter. The question is, Will it stand critical examination? Or will the Jesus hope prove upon critical assessment to be just as empty as Fellini's Martians?

Fortunately we are provided with a considerable amount of evidence to enable us to answer that question. I propose to examine it under three headings: Can we trust the manuscripts? Can we trust the sources? Can we trust the story?

CAN WE TRUST THE MANUSCRIPTS?

I keep bumping into a myth as I chat with students. Someone has told them that the New Testament manuscripts are late and therefore unreliable, and have been heavily tampered with over the years. The notion has a very interesting origin. In 1842 a German theologian, Bruno Bauer, was deprived of his chair because of his wildly unorthodox opinions. That greatly influenced Karl Marx, who surmised that he had been scandalously wronged by the religious establishment, who did not dare allow the shaky foundations of their house of faith to be impartially investigated. It was Bauer's view that Jesus never lived, but was a figment of the imagination of the evangelist Mark.

Marx never examined Christian origins for himself. Indeed, he was willfully blind to the historical evidence. Instead, he uncritically swallowed the absurd theory put forward by Bauer and argued that Christianity arose in the second century A.D. as a revolt of the masses; Jesus was a mythological figure, and nobody tried to claim his historicity until the latter part of the second century when the New Testament was written—itself a historically worthless account.

This view of Bauer, modified by Marx, has many times been decisively refuted. But it has had enormous influence through Marx's writings and the subsequent communist takeover. It is one of the ironies of history (and a judgment on liberal Protestantism) that the vagaries of a politically incorrect theologian and the sharp reaction of the orthodox should have laid the spiritual foundation for the most powerful atheistic regime the world has ever experienced.

The truth is very different. We are better placed to assess the reliability of the manuscript tradition in the case of the New Testament than of any other ancient book. No ancient document has come down to us with such a wealth of manuscript tradition as the Gospels. We have copies of them going back to well within a century of their composition in the latter part of the first century A.D. Now that is fantastic compared with classical authors of the period. The gap, for example, between when Tacitus wrote (about fifty years after the Evangelists) and the earliest surviving manuscript of his work is some eight hundred years. With the historian Livy, a near contemporary of the Evangelists, the gap is eleven hundred years. In striking contrast to the two or three manuscripts we have attesting the text of these secular writers, we have literally hundreds of the New Testament. They are written in many languages, and they come from all over the ancient world. They give us the text of the New Testament with astonishing unanimity (just as the Isaiah scrolls found at Qumran precisely confirm the text of our previous earliest manuscript of Isaiah, though they antedate it by more than a thousand years). Of course, there are many variant readings in this vast array of manuscripts, all copied laboriously by hand. But those who have studied the subject would all agree on these two central points.

First, no single doctrine of the New Testament depends on a disputed reading.

And second, the text of the New Testament is so certain that no competent scholar would dream of making a conjectural emendation (i.e., a guess about what the text *should* read), common though that is in the case of classical texts. The strength of the manuscript tradition makes such a procedure impossible.

We actually possess (in Manchester, of all places!) a fragment of the Gospel of John that experts date between A.D. 100 and 125. And it is now very probable that we have a fragment of Mark's Gospel, hidden in one of the caves at Qumran, which dates back to before A.D. 68 when the community was overrun by the Romans and the cave sealed up. As I write, there is ferment in the scholarly world over a papyrus fragment of Matthew's Gospel, which a leading papyrologist is dating about

A.D. 60. We have all four Gospels in papyrus books well before A.D. 200. A document called *The Unknown Gospel* was discovered some years ago, written before A.D. 150. It draws heavily on our four Gospels and so shows the authoritative position they had already attained by that time. The early heretic Valentinus, whose *Gospel of Truth,* written about A.D. 130, also turned up a few decades ago, quoted the New Testament writings extensively. So did the church fathers Polycarp and Clement of Rome, thirty or forty years earlier.

By the end of the first century, that is to say within the lifetime of some who had known Jesus, the New Testament was not only written, but it was on the way to being collected. And from the outset it was seen as authoritative information about Jesus. So authoritative that the Christians quoted it with the same reverence that they gave to the Old Testament. So authoritative that the heretics knew they must quote it extensively if they were going to get a hearing for their heresies.

All of that enabled Professor Frederic Kenyon, the celebrated biblical archaeologist, to conclude, "The interval between the dates of the original composition and the earliest extant evidence becomes so small as to be negligible, and the last foundation for any doubt that the Scriptures have come down to us substantially as they were written has now been removed" (*The Bible and Archaeology,* 288).

CAN WE TRUST THE SOURCES?

Although most of what we know about Jesus is contained in Christian writings, there is corroboration from non-Christian sources, and it will be convenient to begin with them. They are certainly not prejudiced in favor of the Christian cause!

The Non-Christian Sources

First, there is the evidence from early Roman writers. There is not a lot of it. You would not expect wealthy men of letters in Rome to take a great deal of notice of a carpenter who lived for a few years in Judea, on the edge of the map. What there is, however, is remarkable.

Tacitus, the great historian of the early empire, wrote his *Annals* at the very beginning of the second century. In them he gave a careful year-by-year account of affairs in Rome. When he got to the year A.D. 64, when much of Rome was burned down, he made it plain that he agreed with the generally held view that Nero was responsible, because he wanted to redevelop a large area in the center of the city as his palace.

To dispel this rumor, Nero substituted as culprits and treated with the most extreme punishment some people, popularly known as Christians, whose disgraceful activities were notorious. The originator of the name, Christ, had been executed when Tiberius was emperor by order of the procurator Pontius Pilate. But the deadly cult, though checked for a time, was now breaking out again not only in Judea, the birthplace of this evil, but even throughout Rome, where all nasty and disgusting ideas from all over the world pour in and find a ready following. (*Annals* 15.44)

Obviously Tacitus did not know a lot about Christians. He did not like them, but he was clear they did not burn down Rome. He had a basic knowledge of "the originator of the name" who was born in Judea, lived under the principate of Tiberius (A.D. 14–37), and was executed by Pilate (who governed the province A.D. 26–36). Tacitus knew there were lots of Christians in Rome as early as the sixties.

More came from Pliny the Younger, a contemporary of Tacitus, who was sent in A.D. 112 to govern Bithynia in northern Turkey. He kept referring everything to Emperor Trajan, and the correspondence survives. He wrote one long letter about Christians (*Letters* 10.96).

They were spreading like wildfire in his province. Christianity was becoming a social and economic problem. The pagan temples were closing down for lack of customers, the sacred festivals were becoming deserted, and the demand for sacrificial animals had ceased. So Pliny executed those who refused to renounce their Christian allegiance. But he had qualms about it. That was why he wrote to Trajan.

He had discovered that nothing improper went on in the Christian assemblies. Their whole guilt lay in refusing to worship the imperial statue and images of the gods, and in their habit of meeting on a fixed day, Sunday, to sing hymns to Christ as God. Their lives, he wrote, were exemplary. You would not find fraud, adultery, theft, or dishonesty among them. And at their common meal they ate food of an ordinary and innocent kind. That is no doubt an allusion to the fact that Christians spoke of "feeding on Christ" in the Communion: to the uninitiated it could sound like cannibalism.

To be sure, Pliny told us nothing specific about Jesus himself. But he was clear that the "Jesus movement" was a major force in the upland province adjoining the Black Sea. This secular governor gave testimony to the quality of life among the Christians, their weekly worship of Christ as God, their unwillingness to accord that status to others (even the emperor), their innocence, and their phenomenal spread.

Writers of the stature of Pliny and Tacitus make the historicity of Jesus certain and confirm some of the evidence we find laid out at much greater length in the Gospels.

We also find references to Jesus in Jewish literature of the time. The most remarkable came from a Jewish guerrilla commander, Flavius Josephus, who fought the invading Romans in the war from A.D. 66 to 70, and subsequently turned historian and tried to restore the reputation of his countrymen and -women in Roman eyes. He told us a little about characters we find in the Gospels: Herod, Caiaphas, John the Baptist, James "the brother of the so-called Christ." But most significant of all was his extended reference to Jesus himself. It is worth quoting in full:

And there arose about this time [he means Pilate's time as governor, A.D. 26–36] Jesus, a wise man if indeed one should call him a man. For he was the performer of astonishing deeds, a teacher of those who are happy to receive the truth. He won over many Jews and also many Greeks. He was the Christ. And when Pilate had condemned him to the cross at the instigation of our own leaders, those who had loved him at first did not give up. For he appeared to them on the third day alive again, as the holy prophets had foretold, and had said many other wonderful things about him. And still to this day the race of Christians, so called after him, has not died out. (*Antiquities* 18.3.3)

Needless to say, such powerful attestation from so hostile a source as Josephus is amazing, and it has attracted enormous suspicion from those who cannot believe it to be genuine. But this testimony, in full, is to be found in all the surviving manuscripts of Josephus, and Eusebius read it there in the fourth century A.D. No doubt some of it is sarcastic: "If indeed one should call him a man" might be a snide allusion to his divine claims. "He was the Christ" might allude to the charge affixed to his cross, "Jesus of Nazareth, Jewish Messiah." But it remains a solid, textually reliable reference to the founder of Christianity by Josephus (himself a late contemporary of Jesus). It alludes to his messiahship, his wisdom, his teaching, his miracles, his many conversions, his death and resurrection—not to mention the continuation of the movement.

Jewish, Roman, and archaeological sources provide a good many more scraps of information about Jesus, but this is not the moment to go into them, except perhaps to summarize what they tell us. We learn that Jesus was born of a virgin, performed miracles, and was executed by Pilate on the cross, in thick darkness, at Passover time. We learn that he had claimed to be God, and that he would depart and come again. He was the Christ. He rose from the tomb. He had disciples, who worshiped him as God.

His movement spread rapidly throughout the Roman world within a generation. His essential message could be distilled in this cryptogram, *ichthus,* meaning "fish." It stood for *Jesus Christ, Son of God, Savior.*

The Christian Sources

Very well, you may say, but what about the Christian evidence in the Gospels? Can we trust it? There are good reasons to suppose we can.

First, no books in all the world's literature have been scrutinized so sharply over two and a half centuries as the Gospels. Today their credibility stands as high as ever. They emerge from every test with the utmost credit. That is an excellent reason for taking with the utmost seriousness the portrait they offer us of Jesus.

Second, there is a remarkable harmony in the general picture they present—as different from second-century imitations as chalk is from cheese. This is not only the case between the Gospels themselves, but between them and the pattern of the early preaching as we learn it from the Acts and from traces in other parts of the New Testament. Such unplanned harmony between authors who had their own viewpoints and were not in collusion gives us great confidence in the report they give us. These Gospel writers were not making it up. They were telling us what happened.

Third, what we read in the Gospels fits closely with the secular evidence sketched in this chapter. But of course, it fills it out and puts flesh on it. What is more, it chimes in precisely with what Paul, the great apostle, told us in his scattered references to the historical Jesus. Paul wrote in the fifties and the early sixties, before the earliest of the Gospels. His allusions are all the more impressive because they are so casual. He was not trying to prove anything or teach his readers new things about Jesus. He was simply reminding them of what they had heard when they first became Christians some years earlier. It would hardly be possible to have better or earlier supporting evidence for the trustworthiness of the Gospels.

Fourth, the survival of eyewitnesses of Jesus' ministry is an important factor to bear in mind when we are assessing the reliability of the Gospels. If the Gospel writers had been telling exaggerated stories about what Jesus did and said, there were still plenty of people around at the time of their publication who could have pointed out the errors. And in that case the Gospels would not have gained the universal circulation and recognition that they did. The eyewitnesses could not fault the records. They were reliable.

There are other ways of checking the trustworthiness of these remarkable little books. If the church had cooked up the contents of the Gospels, we should have expected them to put into Jesus' mouth statements about matters of burning concern to themselves. On the contrary we find that these issues (such as the lordship of Jesus, the gifts of the Holy Spirit, the controversy over the place of circumcision, and whether Christians should eat food that had been offered to idols) are conspicuous by their absence. That gives me a lot of confidence that the Gospel writers were giving a true record and not making up things that would have suited them.

The parables provide another very interesting insight into the reliability of the Gospel writers. People sometimes wonder if these parables go back to Jesus himself or whether the early Christians made them up. But why should anyone have pretended that Jesus taught in such a remarkable way if he did not? Who could have been the genius to create them if not he? One thing is very clear. Although some rabbinic examples exist, nobody before him had taught in parables like Jesus. And nobody after him was able to do so, either. The early church did not preach in parables; but they knew, and faithfully recorded, that Jesus had done so.

There are two critical tools of which the New Testament scholars are rightly fond. One they call the "criterion of multiple attestation." It simply means that there is added reason to accept the authenticity of some event or saying if it is recorded in more than one strand of the gospel tradition. Very well, apply that to the astounding story of Jesus feeding five thousand people from a few rolls and sardines. It is in all four Gospels. You could not have more impeccable evidence for even something so amazing as that. It is not the evidence about Jesus that is at issue, but whether we will go where the evidence points us.

The other tool is the matter of Aramaic. That was the language of Palestine in Jesus' day; Jesus habitually used it. The Aramaic experts have discovered a remarkable thing. Much of the teaching of Jesus can easily be translated back from the Greek into the underlying Aramaic, and then it falls into rhyming cadences. This is very rare and very beautiful. It is also very memorable.

That may account for the close verbal similarity, even identity, that we find in some of Jesus' teaching as recorded in different Gospels. Jews learned by memorizing, and the rhyming Aramaic that underlies parts of our Gospels (and occasionally peeps out in words like *talitha cumi* and *abba*) is highly memorable. No doubt Jesus taught in this way because he wanted his teaching to be carefully remembered and accurately passed on. We have every reason to believe that it was.

CAN WE TRUST THE STORY?

But granted that the story of Jesus was reliably transmitted, can we believe it? That is the problem. Sublime the story certainly is, but is it credible? I suppose the heart of our problem resolves itself into two main questions: Was Jesus more than man? And did he rise from the grave? Let us take the two in turn. Fortunately there is no lack of evidence.

Was Jesus More Than Man?

The Jews, the original people among whom Jesus walked and talked, were passionate monotheists, the people most difficult in all the world to convince that he was more than man. Yet vast numbers of them became convinced. I think these seven elements proved decisive for them— as they could be for us.

First, his character. It has dominated humankind from that day to this, appealing equally to men and women, young and old, all types and nationalities. He combined all the qualities we normally associate with a man and a woman. He had all the virtues known to humankind and none of the vices. There was something magnetically attractive about that life of his, as you will sense if you read a Gospel through with an open mind. For instance, he treated women and children with a welcome and respect unparalleled in antiquity. Men left their work to flock around him. What was there in his heredity and environment that could explain such a character?

Second, his teaching. It is the most wonderful the world has ever known. Nothing like it has emerged before or since. Its profundity, its pungency, its clarity, its authority, set it apart from all other teaching. How do you explain that in a wandering carpenter?

Third, his lifestyle. He taught the highest standards of conduct, and, unlike any other human being before or since, he kept them. He never needed to apologize to people or to God. That is utterly unique. He claimed to be without sin, the inner failure that stains all the rest of us. Every strand of the New Testament shows that his followers, who knew him intimately, agreed.

And remember the French proverb, "No man is a hero to his valet." This man was! Even his enemies, Judas, Pilate, Caiaphas, and the Pharisees, could throw no mud at him that stuck.

Fourth, his miracles. They are not embarrassments to Christians. They are added indications of who he was. These miracles are embedded in almost all strands of the tradition about Jesus, reaching back as it does to within a few years of his life. There is Jewish attestation as well. It is fascinating to contrast people's credulity about ETs and UFOs with their skepticism about the miracles of Jesus that are so firmly documented. The miracles were done for the benefit of others, never for selfish ends. They were no mere mighty deeds: they illustrated and underlined his claims. For instance, when he fed the multitude, he wanted people to realize that he was and is the real nourishment for our lives. When he healed a blind man, he wanted to show them that he could open eyes that are spiritually blind. Similarly when he raised a man from death, it was to underline his claim to be "the resurrection and the life." His miracles do not by themselves prove his deity, but they are highly congruous with it.

Fifth, his fulfillment of prophecy. Literally scores of Old Testament prophecies and predictions found their fulfillment in Jesus of Nazareth. There is no parallel to that anywhere in the history of the world. Different Old Testament concepts, such as Son of man, Son of God, the inaugurator of the final basis of agreement between God and people, the anointed prophet, priest, and king, and many more, intersect in him and in him alone. He is even portrayed as the replacer of the Jewish Law and the embodiment of the glory of God that was in the temple of Solomon long ago. Many of the prophecies concerned his birth and his death—and those are the two hardest areas in which to fake fulfillment. His birth from a virgin, at Bethlehem; his death, despised and rejected, among criminals, undertaken to deal with human sins, followed by burial in a rich man's tomb, crowned by resurrection and ascent to the throne of God—who could arrange a schedule to fulfill all that?

Sixth, his claims. They are outrageous, indeed mad, if they are not true. Despite his personal humility and simplicity of life, he made claims that no other man has ever dared to make. He claimed that God was his "Abba" (an utterly unique filial relationship, like "daddy"), and that whoever had seen him had seen the Father. He claimed the right to forgive human sins, to be worshiped, to be the final judge of humankind, to be the way to God, the truth about God, and the very life of God embodied in human flesh. What are we to make of such claims?

Finally, his death. It is the most famous death in the world. Millions carry the reminder of it in a cross around their neck. Jesus did not, like some modern religious fundamentalists, court martyrdom. He sweated blood at the prospect of death. Yet the unselfishness of that death, its self-sacrifice, its sin bearing, its triumph, drew all sorts of people to him and still does. The fact that so perfect a person went willingly to such a terrible death, coupled with the interpretation that he gave it (to liquidate the sins of the whole world), convinced them. It lent enormous force to Jesus' question: "Who do you say that I am?"

Did Jesus Rise from the Dead?

But what about the Resurrection? The Christian claim hangs, to a large extent, upon its truth or falsehood. How are we to approach what is on the face of it a preposterous claim? We must come at it with an open mind. That is vital. The Christian tends to say, "It is in the Bible. That's good enough for me." The skeptic is inclined to say, "Dead men don't come back." Both Christian and doubter must lay aside prejudice and look at the evidence. It seems to me that five facts cohere and all point in the same direction.

First, Jesus was dead. The point would not be worth making were it not for wild assertions sometimes made that he was not really dead, but was revived in the cool of the tomb and then persuaded his followers of his resurrection. This claim is frankly incredible. No one survived a Roman crucifixion; they were experts at the macabre form of execution. And in John's Gospel we are given a fascinating bit of eyewitness testimony: it says, "One of the soldiers pierced his side with a spear, and at once out came blood and water" (19:34). The writer could not possibly have known the medical importance of his statement. But the separation of dark clot from clear serum is one of the strongest proofs of death. There can be no doubt that Jesus was dead.

Second, the tomb was empty. This is agreed all around. By Easter morning the body of Jesus was absent from the tomb in which he had been laid to rest on Friday. Who could have wanted to remove the body and so give substance to the resurrection story? The only possible people would be his enemies or his friends. I ask you, would his enemies, who had spent three embarrassing years trying to get him put away, remove his body from the grave once they had, at last, gotten him where they wanted? Of course not. Then what about his friends? I don't see how they could. There were a guard of soldiers on the tomb and a massive rock over the entrance—sealed, for good measure. Read about it in Matthew 27:62–66. What is more, his followers would never have done such a thing, even if they could. It is psychologically impossible. Like all Jews, they believed that there would be a resurrection of everyone at the Day of Judgment, but not before. Dispirited at the execution of the One on whom they had pinned their hopes, they scattered to their homes after his death. They were certainly not expecting his resurrection. It is sometimes suggested that they were guilty of deliberate fraud, stealing the body and then pretending Jesus was alive again. That is beyond belief. They went around the Roman world for the rest of their lives boldly proclaiming the Resurrection, despite appalling obstacles. They allowed themselves to be persecuted, imprisoned, and killed for maintaining its truth. You don't go through all that for a fraud!

Third, the Christian church was born. It can be traced back to that first Easter. Something got it off the ground with enormous power and joy and confidence a few days after the execution of its founder. If not the Resurrection, would you like to hazard a credible alternative? Initially there was nothing to distinguish them from the rest of Judaism apart from their burning conviction that Jesus was the long-awaited Messiah and had conquered death. It was the faith that set the entire Roman world ablaze. Their three major innovations of baptism, the Communion, and Sunday are all incomprehensible without the Resurrection. In baptism you entered into the death of Christ as you went into the water, and into the new realm of his resurrection as you emerged. At the Communion you did not merely look back to the death of a hero (as the Greek memorial feasts did). You celebrated a meal, which was an anticipation of heaven, with the risen, though invisible, Jesus himself! As for Sunday, that was amazing. Jews had for centuries kept Saturday as a special day because it commemorated the completion of God's work of creating the world (Gen. 2:2; Ex. 20:8). But gradually "the first day of the week," i.e., Sunday, replaced Saturday as the weekly day of celebration. It brought to mind not so much the creation of the world, but its potential re-creation through the resurrection of Jesus Christ. It opened a new door of hope for humankind.

Fourth, Jesus appeared extensively to his followers after his death. We have many accounts of the resurrection appearances of Jesus. Over a period of forty days he appeared to a wide variety of people in a wide variety of settings: the disciples; James, his unbelieving brother; Thomas the skeptic; Mary Magdalene, his friend; Mary, his mother; and no less than five hundred people at one time. Finally he appeared to Saul of Tarsus, his determined enemy, and revolutionized his life. Read the accounts in Matthew 28, Mark 16, Luke 24, John 20–21, and 1 Corinthians 15:1–11, which is the earliest of them all. Read, and make up your own mind. Could these be hallucinations? Hallucinations do not happen to different groups in different places at different times. Moreover, they tend to be a mark of disintegration of the personality. But the resurrection appearances marked a new wholeness, a new confidence and joy, a new outreach in the disciples who had witnessed them. Read the Acts of the Apostles and see the sequel for yourself.

Finally, the crunch point. *Lives were transformed by meeting this risen Jesus, and they still are.* Think of Peter, changed from a coward and a turncoat at the Crucifixion when he deserted Jesus to a man of rock on whose courage and witness the early church was founded. Think of Saul of Tarsus, who met with the risen Jesus on the road to Damascus when he was on a mission to destroy Christians. He became the most passionate and intelligent Christian missionary the world has ever seen. Think of the disciples as a group. They had deserted Jesus in his hour of need, but after the first Easter they were prepared to take on all and sundry as they contended for the Resurrection that had turned them from a rabble into a church. Or think of James, the brother of Jesus, who had been very skeptical about him during his lifetime, but subsequently became the leader of the Jerusalem church. What made the difference? It was the Resurrection. "He appeared to James" (1 Cor. 15:7).

When you consider honestly and soberly the change in the lives of these people, and of millions since all over the world from every background and nationality and culture; when you consider that they all put their transformation down to the Resurrection; when you reflect on the remarkable fact that they did not simply claim that he rose from death but is alive today and they know him and communicate with him—then I think you will agree that we have very strong evidence that the resurrection story is true, and that Christ is a mighty force to be reckoned with today.

I received a letter some time ago from a person who had been helped by something I had written on the resurrection of Jesus. She said,

> Your book opened the eyes of the most doubting
> Thomas there ever was. Thank you for writing so
> clearly about the resurrection. I had known about it

since childhood, but the penny has only just dropped, and I'm nearly fifty.

Why, oh why, isn't the resurrection *shouted* out in our churches every Sunday? This is the good news I have been looking for for so long. I had always thought that the good news was the forgiveness of sins—and it didn't make much sense and certainly I wasn't very grateful. This is far, far more.

It is indeed. I reckon the resurrection of Jesus is the best news ever brought to humankind—by the real extraterrestrial. What do you think?

6

Delusions

THE WESTERN WORLD HAS BEEN BEDEVILED BY A SERIES of fashionable isms, such as communism (currently a bit passé), individualism, subjectivism, deconstructionism, and the rest. But none are more insidious than materialism, relativism, and pluralism. Let's have a look at them and see how they stand scrutiny in the light of the facts we established in the last chapter.

MATERIALISM

Materialism is the governing philosophy of the twentieth century. We are preoccupied with money, whether we are poor or rich. We are captivated by the passion to possess more and more things. Slogans like "Greed, that's what will rebuild this nation" and "He who dies with the most toys wins" reveal the direction of our society very clearly. Who says you can't have it all—with an

American Express card? The consumer mentality has caught on around the globe. Look at what has happened in Russia since the collapse of communism—all the worst forms of Western materialism. If there is one article of faith that marks the late twentieth century, it is the conviction of our inalienable right to have more and more. Shopping has become the country's favorite pastime. With apologies to Descartes, it could be said, "I shop, therefore I am," or, if you like, "Tesco, ergo sum." Gone is the idealism of the sixties and early seventies. The main goal of the contemporary scene is financial success and a measure of security. Money has become a way of defining who we are by what we possess. When there are no values, money counts. Indeed, it counts so much that it has become a form of worship.

You can understand something of the beliefs and priorities of the people of the Middle Ages by the soaring cathedrals they left behind them. You can understand a great deal about modern society from the shopping malls, which are our cathedrals to consumerism and affluence. At the end of World War II there were just eight shopping malls in the whole of America. Between 1970 and 1990 another twenty-five thousand sprang into being. The biggest in the world is the West Edmonton Shopping Mall. Apart from its 828 shops and 110 restaurants it has all manner of leisure activities. There are a mammoth theme park with wave pool, a roller coaster, submarines, dolphins, a life-size galleon, and a plastic whale. Shopping has become an all-consuming activity. You can easily spend a whole day in a mall like this. It has become a way of life. And these malls are becoming increasingly common in Great Britain. "Shopping malls, megacenters and commercial blocks are the temples of the new age," writes Mike Starkey in *Born to Shop*.

> Speedbank machines are the wayside shrines where we perform our ritual devotions to the god which motivates us. The icons which offered medieval people the ultimate choice in life have given way to the shelves offering the ultimate in consumer choices. . . . In an earlier age life's adversity was met by a robust faith, even if it was only in human nature. Today we have our own solution. When the going gets tough, the tough go shopping. (P. 83)

The Emptiness of Materialism

When we stop to look at the matter critically, it is hard not to agree that materialism is a peculiarly dangerous ideology. It is *false,* for one thing. People matter more than things, and people get squeezed out when economics are king. A good example of that is the true-life TV series *Hollywood Kids,* showing the emotional deprivation and inner emptiness of the poor rich children of film stars who have subordinated family relationships to the quest for fame and money. They are not unique. A great many people in Great Britain today feel their parents offer them toys but not time, and they are impoverished.

There's another problem. Materialism is *addictive.* The more you have, the more you want. The Romans had a motto about it: "Money is like seawater. The more you drink, the thirstier you become." Or as the economist Lord Keynes put it, "Avarice and greed must remain our gods for a little longer still."

What is more, materialism undoubtedly *hardens our sympathies.* Once we have settled for making money and possessions our priority, other people become secondary. Our own society is notably less compassionate than it was when the pursuit of wealth was less central to our aims. Great Britain has become two nations, the poor North and the wealthy South, and there are certainly similar divides in the great American urban centers. And we do not care. We see terrible tragedies such as Rwanda and Bosnia on TV, and we shrug our shoulders. Just too bad. In our lifetime we have seen two poisonous fruits of materialism. We have known the iron, unacceptable face both of communism and of consumerism. Surely there must be a better way to live than either of those?

Then there is a fundamental aspect to human nature that a materialistic lifestyle reveals as nothing else does. It is the paradox of hedonism: the pursuit of pleasure is *self-defeating*. There is in the human heart an emptiness that nothing transient can fill. I am sure you have felt it in your life—the emptiness that comes with Christmas afternoon! The richest people in the world feel it too. Paul Getty Sr., the wealthiest man in his generation, had five marriages. He did not marry a sixth time because an astrologer told him, "You will only live a short time after a sixth marriage," and he wanted to be a hundred. That, by the way, was when he was eighty-four. He lived in a house protected by dogs. He was terrified of solitude but equally terrified by people. He lived to work. The world's richest man was bankrupt inside. He is no exception. Sinead O'Connor, the celebrated singer, was blunt about it: "As a race we feel empty. That is because our spirituality has been wiped out. . . . As a result we fill that gap with alcohol, drugs, sex, or money."

No, materialism does not satisfy, and *it does not last*. To rely on wealth is most unwise. A collapse in the stock market can wipe it all away overnight. Unemployment stalks the land, and it can strike in the boardroom as sharply as it does on the shop floor. Illness can remove all pleasure in our vaunted possessions. And to travel in a developing country makes us profoundly aware of the injustice in the distribution of wealth and shames us for our greed. To reflect on what consumerism is doing to our planet is an important warning against the perils of materialism and regarding the constant growth of the GNP as the goal of economics. Madness lies that way— the depletion of the remaining rain forests, ozone destruction, global warming, water and ground pollution, and the rapidly shrinking size of the very finite cake of which we all want larger and larger slices. The acquisitive appetite that we have let loose in our Western societies has turned around to destroy us.

In fact, materialism destroys not only our environment but also ourselves. It is highly *destructive* of all that is best in our characters and often leads to envy, lust, luxury, greed, murder, and suicide. It undermines what is true and beautiful in us, and acts like a slow poison. As G. K. Chesterton put it so forcefully: "A person who is dependent upon the luxuries of this life is a corrupt person, spiritually corrupt, politically corrupt, financially corrupt. Christ said that to be rich is to be in a peculiar danger of moral wreck."

A Much-Needed Alternative

Those words of Chesterton's bring us face-to-face with Jesus and his standard for life. It was said of him by one of his early followers, "Though he was rich, yet for our sake he became poor, so that we through his poverty might become rich." The writer went on to speak of the riches of character, of generosity, of love that Christ brings about in his followers. It is very attractive. Think of the riches Jesus shared with his heavenly Father: he was, as I argued in the last chapter, the Source, the Sustainer, and the goal of the whole universe, and yet he became a human being—to reach us in our spiritual blindness and our chains. Born not to a wealthy family but in a working-class home. Not in a palace but in a stable. He lived a life not of luxury, but of honest manual labor followed by a few years of preaching and healing. He had no regular home, no wife and family, no resources apart from his selfless character. And yet he was profoundly happy.

Does that not shame our lust for possessions? His whole life was a protest against materialism. A man's life, he maintained, does not consist in the multitude of his possessions. And he told a marvelous story to back it up. There was a rich entrepreneur whose farming had been particularly successful. He was planning massive expansion, with a view to settling down in due course to a luxurious retirement. "But God said to him, 'You fool, tonight you are going to die. And then all the things you have prepared—whose will they be?'" A heart attack carried him off in the night—and all the baubles he had spent his life amassing were left for someone else. Fool indeed!

Money has become the opiate of the people. The obsessive pursuit of wealth is a modern pathology. We need a far bigger and richer vision than personal consumerism. Economics is no proper indicator of who we are. We need to recover the qualities of compassion, self-discipline, and generosity. The greed of the rich must be tempered by the need of the poor. We must take care of our planet; it is the only one we have. We must manage it, not ruin it. And above all we must regain the respect for others as people, made in the image of God, not mere means to our gratification. The New Testament offers us such a vision. It can become a reality when Jesus Christ is made number one.

One of the most powerful statements on this subject in recent years has been made by Alexander Solzhenitsyn. The elderly man who learned his wisdom in a prison camp was addressing the wealthy young students who had gained their laurels at Harvard. At the Graduation Address in 1978 this was his advice:

> If humanism were right in declaring that man is born to be happy, he would not be born to die. Since his body is doomed to die his task on earth . . . must be of a more spiritual nature. It cannot be the unrestrained enjoyment of everyday life. It cannot be the search for the best ways to obtain material goods and then cheerfully to get the most out of them. It has to be the fulfillment of a permanent earnest duty so that one's life journey may become an experience of moral growth, so that one may leave life a better human being than when one started it.

Solzhenitsyn found the key to that transformation in Jesus Christ. He made a thoughtful, well-considered choice. Was he right?

RELATIVISM

We were sitting in a restaurant having lunch and discussing morals. "It was so much easier when I was young," said my friend. "We knew what was right, even though we didn't always do it." Not so today. We make up our morality as we go along. There's no such thing as right, only what seems right to me. And that may be very different from what seems right to you.

Relativism holds enormous influence these days. Indeed, it is almost taken for granted. It makes few moral demands on us because we can reduce our standards to what we feel disposed to do. It allows us to ditch almost every virtue in the book, if we so wish, apart from tolerance; to breach that is the ultimate sin because tolerance justifies my doing what I want and not being blamed for it. Not only is it very appealing, but it accords with the enormous variety of cultures that jostle together in our streets. You do your thing. I'll do mine. But don't bug me. What's wrong with that?

Objections to Relativism

A lot is wrong with it. First and foremost, it doesn't make sense. Wonderfully liberating, no doubt, to cry, "There are no absolute standards. Everything is relative." But nonsense just the same. Because the person who makes this claim clearly expects us to accept it as the *truth*! Everything must be thought of as relative except the claim that everything is relative. That relativist argument claims absolute status. The claim is totally bogus.

But there are far more serious objections to relativism. To make your standards up at your own preference leads inexorably to the breakdown of society. We are seeing it in our countries today when crime has risen to the highest level ever, especially among young offenders. They feel good about stealing a car, driving it at 100 miles an hour, and then burning it. Some them have been arrested three or four hundred times, but nothing can be done. They are too young to be imprisoned even in a juvenile institution. It drives the police mad. Only yesterday there were three young boys and a girl who had broken into the house of an aged man suffering from cancer and cut his face to pieces, killing him and reveling in it. That is an extreme case of relativism in ethics for you, but it is becoming increasingly common. A friend's daughter was offered drugs the first day she went to school. Someone thought it right.

Lies and sleaze are commonplace in business and politics. Trust is collapsing. The word of the great companies and institutions used to be their bond. Not now. You don't need me to say more about it; it is only too obvious that if everyone does his or her own thing, there is going to be more and more societal chaos. Ron Bibby, the Canadian sociologist, describes the situation graphically in his book about Canadian society in two words: *mosaic madness*. Individualism run riot. No cohesion. That is what happens if you have no objective norms.

And relativism leads to unalloyed selfishness, destructive to others and also to ourselves. The French have a term for it, *anomie*. It is the malaise widespread in society—a sense of lostness, an emotional sickness that comes from living without guidelines. It is alienation that is so marked a characteristic of our day. "Money, success, it's all meaningless. I'm dead inside. I feel a thousand years old. I am bored with so much, even with my money." That was Lyle Stewart, a pornography baron, but it might well have been written by any other successful person. As Noel Coward put it in one of his plays, "The past depresses me, the present bores me, and the future scares me to death."

Three Influential Writers

On the larger scale, the dangers of relativism are very obvious. If there are no objective moral standards restraining people and nations, they are free to do what they want. "Is there no God? Then everything is permitted." That is how Dostoyevsky saw it in *The Brothers Karamazov*. He was right. That is how atheistic communists acted in Russia when they raped Czechoslovakia and Afghanistan. That was the philosophy of the Nazis when they decided to go for a pure Aryan race and liquidate six million Jews. And do you remember the attitude of the Nazi war criminals when brought to trial? "I was just following orders."

A century ago the atheist Friedrich Nietzsche saw very clearly that if God and traditional values were eliminated, the strong could impose their will on the rest. That led him to the model of the superman and the ethic of the will-to-power. This century has been playing out that scenario, in Russia and Germany, Serbia and Vietnam. Ours has been the bloodiest century in all history. Maybe William Penn was right: "Nations must be governed by God or they will be ruled by tyrants." History has yet to produce a single example of relativism providing enlightened and benevolent government. And if it is not good for the state, it can't be good for the individual, however seductive it appears.

One of the most powerful and perceptive books of this century is William Golding's *Lord of the Flies*. In it he shows the disastrous, indeed murderous, results of human nature unrestrained by any objective morals—even when that nature belongs to a bunch of schoolchildren. Relativism in morals simply will not do. It is the recipe for chaos. And it is certainly not something that is self-evidently correct. Far from it. The nations of the world do not just go for any old values. They are remarkably agreed-upon virtues that they accept as valid and try to promote: bravery, honesty, marital fidelity, care for children, politeness—all these are qualities recommended in practically every culture and religion. It is flying in the face of all the evidence to suppose that moral relativism is the route to progress. It is the way to extinction.

The Ultimate Refutation

In Jesus of Nazareth we have the supreme example of a life that displays all the virtues known to human beings and none of the vices. His life has been the inspiration for most of the best art, music, medicine, and character down the succeeding two millennia. Are we to trash it and say that, in the light of relativism and its current political correctness, it is a matter of indifference whether we go for the standards of Jesus or those of Hitler and Stalin? Are we reduced to the moral swamps of relativism? Or is there some solid rock standing out of the morass? Could it be that the Absolute has come into the world of the relative? Could it be that the best of all advice would be to follow his invitation to life at its best, "Come, follow me"? We have the privilege of choosing.

PLURALISM

The Meaning of Pluralism

One of the most pervasive ideologies of our day is pluralism. Let's be clear what we are talking about. All

Western countries are "plural" societies these days, with a variety of cultures, faiths, and races. We must distinguish this plurality from *pluralism*. This ideology makes a fundamental distinction between facts and values. Facts are public, and we are all expected to agree with them— like the date of the Battle of Gettysburg or the existence of Congress. But it is very different with values and beliefs. These are private and very diverse. In this realm there are no norms. You have your views and I have mine. They are all equally valid and equally relative. Certainty in matters of religion is impossible and would be undesirable anyhow because it would prove socially disruptive. All religions lead to God. Sincerity, not truth, is the important thing (anyway, what is truth?). Tolerance is what matters.

Against this background all truth claims are suspect, and none more than the Christian insistence that Jesus is the way to God, the truth about God, and the very life of God. To talk like that is narrow, intolerant, and fanatical. It is clearly untenable. Okay. Let's have a good look at pluralism.

Pluralism Is Not New

It is often suggested that modern thought has rendered historic Christianity untenable—we are too sophisticated to believe that stuff anymore. But a moment's reflection will show that is not the case. As soon as monotheism broke into the world with the ancient Jews, it had to face all the challenges of pluralism. The Canaanites, the Moabites, the Hivites, the Hittites, and all the rest swarmed around the little country of Israel like bees, all with different and usually disgusting beliefs, and sought to swamp Jewish faith in one holy God or else to assimilate it to their own myths. Judaism held out resolutely against both expedients. And the Romans were so amazed at their exclusive monotheism that they gave the Jews special privileges and dispensations not accorded to any other part of the Roman Empire. They realized that the Jews would fight to the death for the truth of their position. Here was a people who believed in truth. It was all rather a shock.

The First Christians Rejected It

It was just the same with the first Christians. They were Jews, every one of them, but they went farther and were utterly persuaded that this one true God had showed his hand—no, his whole being—in the person of Jesus of Nazareth. God had come to seek humankind and draw us back to him. It was no myth or private value judgment. It was sober history and sober truth. Indeed, it was the most important truth in the world. They were clear that there was *one* way of cleansing from human sins and frailties, *one* kingdom of love and loyalty to God into which all nations were invited, *one* way of acceptance depending not on religious pedigree or moral achievement but on the sheer generosity of God—all this they maintained with a fearless courage in the face of a religious pluralism that makes our version look mild.

Naturally they were unpopular. But had they gone for one of the politically correct religious attitudes under the empire, they would not have been persecuted; nobody would have bothered them. The Romans had broad views on religion. When they conquered your territory, they tended either, like the Hindus, to add your special deity to the existing pantheon or else to identify him, as modern pluralists would, with a deity of their own who fulfilled the same function. This the Christians resolutely refused to do. They were convinced that they were onto the truth, and they refused to give it up. That is why they were vilified and spasmodically persecuted. There's nothing new about pluralism. The only new thing is the willingness of some church people to surrender to it.

Of course, it has a growing appeal these days. We have a new global consciousness and a new understanding of other faiths, which are right and proper. But they need not prevent us from firmly and courteously maintaining that pluralism will not do, for a variety of good reasons.

Pluralism Makes Strange Assumptions

Pluralism makes some very strange assumptions. It assumes that *Christians are arrogant* and want to push their views on everybody else. Not so. Christians believe that they have found treasure, and they want to share it with everyone else, modestly but confidently. And that is very different.

It assumes that *Christians think they know it all and everyone else is wrong*. No sensible Christians think that. They are well aware of how little they know—but they do know the Jesus into whose care they have entrusted their lives. They do not for a moment imagine they have a monopoly on truth. They know that there is something good in almost every faith or ideology—otherwise it would never have captured the hearts of human beings. Christians want to trace that good stuff down to its source in the God who put it there and gave a full disclosure of himself in Jesus Christ. Whenever we admire the prayers of Muslims, the respect for life among Buddhists, or whatever, our question must be, "This is great, but what is there here that is not to be found in Christ?" I have yet to find anything.

Another assumption is that *all religions lead to God*. That sounds wonderfully liberal, but it is sheer nonsense all the same. How can all religions lead to God when some of them do not believe in a personal God at all, like Buddhism, while others believe in many gods, like animism? Some believe in an inscrutable deity who cares nothing about the world he set in progress, some believe in a vengeful deity who is out to get us, while Christianity maintains God is personal, loving, and active for our rescue. The whole idea of God is different in these conflicting viewpoints.

Another of the strange assumptions of pluralism is that *sincerity is all you need*. Believe it sincerely, and you will be fine. What an utterly cynical creed! We would not dream of applying it to mathematics, politics, or any other sphere of life. I may sincerely believe that a bottle of whiskey a day is good for me, and act on it, but that will not prevent cirrhosis of the liver. Sincerity is no guarantee of truth. We can be sincere and wrong.

Want another false assumption? It is that *all religious experience is basically the same*. Who says? The Western liberal, of course. But a Muslim fundamentalist killing Christians in northern Nigeria may not be having at all the same religious experience as the animist seeking to buy off evil spirits or the Hindu guru meditating on reality. And if you ask converts from other faiths, they will tell you in no uncertain terms that much as they value their hereditary background, the experience they have of God as Christians is radically different from anything they ever experienced before, particularly in the areas of knowing God personally, having an assurance of forgiveness, and feeling an inner joy and peace they cannot but attribute to the Holy Spirit whom they have welcomed within them.

And you know, it is very arrogant of us Western people to airily dismiss other religions as the same or going in the same direction. Is the satanist following the same path that Mother Teresa followed? Ask the adherents of Islam in the Gulf if all religions lead to God and if it does not much matter which you follow. It is Western liberals who tell us that all religions go the same way, not the adherents of these faiths themselves—still less Jesus of Nazareth. His lifestyle was very humble, but his claims were majestic: he saw himself as bringing God onto the stage of human history, no less. And that is a wildly different claim from that of the founder of any other faith. It is either right or wrong.

Pluralism Is Morally Useless

I have another problem with this fashionable pluralism. It is morally defective. It has no help to offer us with our ethical struggles. Pluralism in belief and relativism in morals go hand in hand. The result is disastrous. Think of the murder and gang rape carried out by the practitioners of satanism. Think of the widow burned alive on her husband's funeral pyre, which was standard Hindu practice until the British came to India and stopped it. Pluralism accepts the vast varieties of ethical standards and religious beliefs available. In keeping with pluralism, you pick and choose and anything goes; it is all okay. It gives you no guiding star and no moral power.

Pluralism Is Afraid of Truth

But worst of all, pluralism is totally allergic to the issue of truth. True believers are the real dangers because they claim to be right. But what if they *are* right? Galileo claimed to be right and was given a terrible time for it by the religious establishment of the day. But he *was* right, and everyone now recognizes as much. What if the Christians are right? What if there is a living God who made the world and all that is in it? What if he does love us so much that he came to reveal himself to us in a human life? What if he did burden himself with our moral filth? What if he does offer the power of his resurrection life to those of any or no faith who will accept it?

There is a massive truth question here, and it will not go away. It didn't go away from Pontius Pilate, either, when Jesus, who had claimed to embody truth, stood before him. "What is truth?" asked the governor, and received no answer. For truth was there in front of him. I have a nasty feeling that Pilate knew it. He, like us, had to make up his mind about it. He could not evade the choice. We all know how he decided.

How will you decide? In this postmodern age we are skeptical of truth claims, disenchanted with past systems and ideologies. We are open to whatever really helps people's daily lives. *Jesus does!* We are open to story, particularly individual story. Well, the Christian has a story to tell of the difference Jesus has progressively made to him or her. What is more, as we saw earlier, it is not merely *my* story. For my story is linked with *his* story, the greatest story ever told. That story makes sense of humankind, our environment, our morals, our hunger for lasting relationship.

Perhaps we were mistaken to exclude the category of truth from our minds? Perhaps Jesus really is the truth—not just for me but for others all over the world? Maybe that is too big a jump for you to take right now. But in any case, what he offers is very attractive. Maybe we should be very suspicious of the materialism, the relativism, and the pluralism that surround us on every side, and see how they match up with the alternative: the man who claims to bring God to us, the One who gives us richly all things to enjoy, but tells us that if we live for possessions, we are fools. The One who brings reality into our history and our lives. The One before whom all rival ideologies pale like candles before the dawn. If that were the case, it would be terrible to miss it. The search is worth it.

The next three chapters will continue this search. It is not too difficult for us. The stress of modern life, the longing for freedom, and the universal hunger for love will give us all the indicators we need if we are to make an informed choice—to follow Jesus Christ or to turn our backs on him.

7

Stress

Not long ago I found myself speaking on the Christian faith at a dinner in Brussels. "What is the issue nearest to people's hearts?" I asked my hosts. "Stress" was the answer. So I decided to speak on stress to a remarkable gathering of people, many of them highly placed in NATO or the European community. It was a surprise to me, but it was clearly the right subject. The local newspaper was thrust into my hands as I arrived, and I found no less than two articles on the subject. The author of one of them was at the dinner.

CAUSES OF STRESS

The causes of stress may intensify in the pressurized life of Brussels, but they are much the same as those that assail us all. Work topped the list. In an age when more and more are unemployed, those in employment have to work much harder. Managers are often at work two hours earlier than they used to be. The fears of unemployment and of ill health were predictably high on the list, as were domestic unhappiness and the strain of moving and changing jobs.

This is what awaits those who are still students. In the meantime they have plenty of hassles to cope with. I have before me a newspaper clipping revealing the staggering fact that one in three students at Cambridge University seeking help from university counselors said that he or she had considered committing suicide. The growing academic, personal, and financial pressures are responsible. Indeed, suicide is second only to automobile accidents as the prime cause of death among young adults.

Some of the strain comes from the sort of people we are. If we are easygoing, satisfied with our jobs or roles in society, not particularly competitive, rarely rushed, slow in eating, walking, and talking, then we are unlikely to be hard hit by stress. The competitive, restless, ambitious person who tries to do too many things at once, is always rushed, is impatient while waiting, anticipates what others are going to say, and is fast in all actions— well, that sort of person is at high risk in the stress stakes. But as we all know, there is a lot more to it than that.

The things that happen to us are at least as significant as our basic characters in inducing stress. Serious injury, the death of a loved one, the breakup of a relationship, change of job or residence, family problems, and debt are among the most stressful.

At universities the most common causes of stress are probably as follows. There are the strain to excel in academics or in sports and the anguish that occurs if that does not work out. Exams are a major time of stress and tragically lead to some suicides every year. Then there is the longing for a deep relationship with a partner— and if and when this relationship is realized, the deeper it is, and the worse it feels when it breaks up, as it often does. Debt is an increasing problem. Not only is this true of society at large, but it has penetrated deep into the student world. With the cutback in grants it is a struggle even to pay the rent and eat cheap meals, and many students get immersed in debt, which they fear it will take years to settle. Then there is worry about the job market. Unemployment is rife, and many graduates do not get a job when they leave universities. Certainly they do not have the wealth of choice that was typical when I was a student. And underneath it all there is often stress because of some trauma in the past that may well remain unacknowledged but is destructive all the same. It may be some abuse they have been subjected to in earlier life, some habit they feel badly about, or some action they profoundly regret. And they don't know what to do about it. That is a component of stress. A student survey was conducted recently, asking, "What do you feel most embarrassed about the morning after a drunken spree?" No less than 41 percent of those questioned replied, "The person I find myself in bed with when I wake up."

Of course, there are many suggestions around of how to handle stress. The journal I referred to in Brussels advocated the following: stop to chat and joke; have a cup of tea, a smoke, a chocolate; listen to music; watch TV; or drink booze. Other suggestions include maximizing your human potential, practicing regular meditation, seeking to acquire more possessions or achievements, and turning to drugs and/or alcohol. But they don't really work.

THE MAN WHO WAS STRESS-FREE

There was once a person who had utter peace. His name was Jesus. In the midst of a storm that threatened to sink the boat we find him in perfect peace. When surrounded by a dangerous riot with folks out for his blood, he displayed precisely the same quality of peace. When almost crushed by people wanting healing, he peacefully attended to them all and then got up extra early the next morning to pray. When he faced the Roman governor who had the power of life and death over him, his peace showed up the inner turbulence of Pilate. Astonishing peace. He never seemed to hurry, but he was never late. He never lost his cool, whatever the provocation. But in three years he did enough to get a third of the human race to claim the Christian label two millennia later! He was notable for his inner peace, whatever the stress.

And the marvelous thing is that he wanted his followers to have this peace of his for themselves. "Peace I leave with you," he said, "My peace I give to you; not as the world gives do I give to you. Let not your heart be troubled, neither let it be afraid" (John 14:27 NKJV). Jesus maintained that real peace is not something we can learn or work for. It is something he gives. And that is an enormously attractive offer. His peace, he told us, is very different from what the world offers. That's just as well because that peace does not run very deep: it depends on our circumstances. But what Jesus offers is a peace that is independent of our circumstances. Something internal, that nothing can take from us unless we permit it. How might we discover it for ourselves?

STRESS FROM PAST REGRETS

Let's begin with the most difficult area. We need to accept God's pardon. That's the crux of the matter. And until we do so, there will be every prospect of stress raising its ugly head from time to time. We were made to live in harmony with God. Being out of harmony with him causes stress. All the stuff we regret but are powerless to change comes up and suffocates us. We may be successful at keeping it under wraps for years, but it will inevitably emerge to damage us.

A great many murderers eventually walk into a police station to give themselves up. They can't live with the strain any longer. I noticed a remarkable example of this in the *Edmonton Journal* in Canada for September 25, 1993. The headline read, "Living a lie: she was on the run from the law for 23 years until she realized she couldn't run away from herself." That was Katherine Ann Power, a 1960s radical student who had driven the getaway car in a deadly bank robbery. Her accomplice had killed a policeman, the father of nine. Not surprisingly, she was on the FBI's most-wanted list for many years. Well, she escaped to Canada, moving from place to place and regularly changing her name. For nearly a decade she lived in Oregon and was known as Alice Metzinger, a professional chef, wife, and mother. One day she held a farewell party for her friends, indicating that she was off to parts unknown. She told them her story. She told them that she could not live with the guilt. And then she gave herself up to the police in Boston. The surrender was cathartic. "Experiencing life without that distorting lens," she wrote, "I am now learning to live with openness and truth, rather than shame and hiddenness."

We all know something of those regrets. There is only one way in the world of getting the past straightened out. It is at the cross of this person who so embodied peace. There he willingly made himself responsible for all the evil in the world. In a way that none of us can fathom, the man who was God burdened himself with the guilt of a whole world that had gone wrong. He carried that terrible burden of our guilt and shame. And he cried, "It is finished." The job was done. From then on the delete key had been pressed on God's computer list of your failures and mine. Gone. It brings incredible release from stress. "Who is a God like you, who pardons sin and forgives? You delight to show mercy" (Mic. 7:18). It is rather like the tide coming in and clearing up all the junk on the seashore, leaving it pristine and clean. Yes, the forgiveness of God is the most wonderful therapy in the world.

You may complain, "These Christians are always going on about the past; it's the present I am interested in." Okay. Let's look at some of the differences Jesus Christ can make in our present problems.

STRESS FROM CIRCUMSTANCES

Take, for example, the stress that comes from facing massive tasks on our own. Peace comes when we recognize that he is with us always, and he is ready to pour his peace into our turbulence. Christianity is not just about the cross where Christ died our death. It is about the Resurrection, which releases him to come and live in our lives. And once we welcome him in, he brings his peace, a peace independent of our circumstances, with him. Our task is to turn to him and ask for it in the midst of whatever is troubling us.

Some years ago the following stressful things happened to me, all within a very short time. I was bereaved of my father. I changed my job, leaving behind a very warm circle of love. I moved across the Atlantic. I was separated from my grown-up children, one of whom was still going through the university. I had to give away my dog. I started in a new country with a new house on a road where I knew nobody. Now that is enough to drive one off the end of the stress meter. But I did not find it like that at all. I shared the whole situation with the Lord, and I found that his peace was a reality, not just God talk.

"You will keep him in perfect peace whose mind is stayed on you, because he trusts in you," sang the prophet (Isa. 26:3). Peace is really a mind-set. It comes from determining to share any crisis and problem with the Lord, who is present with you. "God is our refuge and strength, a very present help in trouble. . . . Be still and know that I am God" (Ps. 46:1, 10). That does not usually remove the crisis, but it brings a deep calm to you and me so that we are able to handle it.

I certainly found that an enormous help as a student in facing major examinations. To know that I could trust God for the outcome that would be for my ultimate good brought a deep sense of peace. Some years ago I worked in Oxford with a large church that had lots of student members. In Oxford you dressed up in black and white in order to take your final exams, which makes you very conspicuous and does little to inspire a sense of calm! Then, if ever, would be the time to panic. But I noticed time and again that our early midweek Communion would be full of students dressed up in this weird outfit, praising God and reveling in his peace, then

snatching a bowl of cornflakes before going along to
the examination schools.

It is much the same with the employment scene.
Fear of unemployment is a frightening harassment. What
if I never get a job? What if I can't keep up the mort-
gage payments? These are terrifying thoughts. Now I
do not want to exaggerate. But the Bible is clear that
God has a plan for our lives. He has prepared good ways
for us to walk in. There may well be a recession, but it
takes more than a recession to wreck God's plans. So I
should be able to trust him, even if I am facing the specter
of unemployment. He has handled it in countless lives
before. He is very experienced at looking after his children. "Trust in the Lord with all your heart and do not
lean to your own understanding. In all your ways acknowledge him, and he will direct your paths" (Prov. 3:5–6).
That is what the Good Book advises. And I have seen
it work in life after life.

We use up so much energy in worrying about things
that we cannot change. What we can change is our attitude. Not to rely on my own understanding, my own
capability to figure it out. But to turn the whole thing
over to the Lord and trust him to bring about his purpose. That could happen in any number of ways. I work
with a friend who was induced to give up his job and

go for a complete change through a phone call. Others see an advertisement in the paper. I think of a friend who became a farm manager as a result of idly reading a tiny advertisement! And the job proved to be one not only that he did with distinction but that also enabled his remarkable pastoral gifts to have full play.

STRESS FROM DEBT

Debt is another massive cause of strain. Does Christ make any difference there? A friend of mine, Rob Parsons, runs a debt-counseling service in Cardiff. He has personally experienced the pain of being trapped in debt. And now he helps others with this problem. He is well aware that not only poverty but also overcommitment can be the cause of debt. And once you are in debt, the sharks take over. He tells of a letter he got from one of the large banks. Since he was "a valued customer," they had generously set aside a loan for him at the "preferential rate" of 20 percent. As he wryly observes: "With friends like that I have no need of enemies. The madness can be summed up in the advertisement which appeared in a national newspaper: 'Now you can borrow enough to get completely out of debt.'" In this credit card age when plastic is so much more convenient than cash, it is all too easy to run into debt.

But the thing that struck me most forcefully from this article of Rob's (*Renewal,* January 1995) was his first reaction once he discovered he was in debt. He knelt down and admitted to God that his own mistakes had gotten him into the mess he was in. He asked God for his pardon and for his wisdom and courage. Then he set about putting the situation right. The sorting out of the problem took some time. But the peace of God was given him at once. Such is the difference Christ makes in this most practical aspect of modern life.

STRESS FROM DISAPPOINTED HOPES

How about the worry that comes with failure to achieve our goals, say in sports or academic life or our jobs? There again the presence of the living Christ, who is always with us and who has a purpose for our lives, makes all the difference. I think I can honestly say that I have known the reality of his peace in all three of those areas—sports, academics, and work.

I recall failing to get a fencing Blue one year at Cambridge when I had been on the team all season and was dropped at the last match. I was certainly fired up—so much so that I beat the England captain that night! But I had something much better than a Blue, the peace of

God that "passes all understanding." People were amazed that I did not go around disgruntled about it. But why should I? I had God's peace setting guard over heart and mind, as the apostle Paul graphically described it.

Or I think of the day when I heard that in the first part of my degree, despite having come so close to a First (similar to graduating magna cum laude) that the examiners discussed it for an hour, I was given a Second. It did not devastate me. I had God's peace in my life. I knew there was a purpose in it. Actually, the purpose was, I am sure, to humble me so that God could use me as he wanted. That turned out to be to lead the Christian Union in the university, and that, in turn, proved invaluable for my future life.

Several times later on in life I missed a prestigious job by a whisker. So what? I knew God was in control of my circumstances, and I claimed his peace. It stuck.

THE RECIPE FOR PEACE

I alluded just now to a remarkable piece in the apostle Paul's letter to the Christians at Philippi. He was writing from prison, and instead of moaning, his letter was full of joy:

Rejoice in the Lord always, and again I say rejoice. Let your calm confidence be seen by one and all. The Lord is at hand. Have no anxiety about anything, but in everything by prayer and supplication let your requests be made known to God. And God's own peace, which passes all understanding, will set guard over your hearts [i.e., feelings] and minds [i.e., thoughts] in Christ Jesus. (Phil. 4:4–7)

Here was a man, lying in prison and expecting that he might well die. But he was utterly at peace. He knew God was in control. And he told us what a difference that makes. First, he realized that worry is positively wrong with such a heavenly Father. So he renounced it: "Have no anxiety about anything." Not only is it wrong, it is stupid. Can worry add a single day to our lives or an inch to our height? Second, he threw his worry, like a heavy sack, on the Lord. Third, he prayed about it, and then instead of taking it away with him, he sensibly left it there. What did he find? That God's own peace set guard over his tumultuous thoughts and worried feelings, as he remained closely linked with Jesus. Faced with stress and pressure he had a choice. He could have recourse to panic or to prayer. He chose prayer. And he got peace. Turn your cares into prayers. That is a marvelous way to reduce stress.

I found that to be true in a severe health crisis. I was leading a mission in Durban, and I suddenly contracted meningitis and was whipped into a hospital. I was semiconscious for the first few days, but I felt the peace of the Lord around me like a warm garment. We had been wondering how to get someone inside that hospital during the mission, and there I was, becoming the rather surprised answer to our prayers! It led to several people discovering Jesus Christ's reality for themselves, particularly some of the doctors and nurses who had so generously looked after me.

A friend came across this hilarious quote in a management book on stress: "I am now going to give you a most important tip—everyone needs an unconditional listener to unload on. Unfortunately there is no human being who is an unconditional listener. So this is what I recommend. Talk to your pet!"

By all means choose that expedient if you wish. It is better than drugs and booze. But there is an alternative: the peace that Jesus gives to those who trust him for it. The Prince of Peace himself invites us: "Come to me, all you who are stressed out and have heavy burdens on your back. I will give you release from all that. Then get into partnership with me and start living my way, and you will discover peace for

your souls" (Matt. 11:28–29). That sort of peace nobody
and no circumstance can take from you. Did Jesus not
promise, "Peace I leave with you, my peace I give to
you"? He meant it.

8

Freedom

THE URGE FOR FREEDOM

THE URGE TO BE FREE IS A FUNDAMENTAL HUMAN impulse. It is one of the milestones in the march of history. You see it in the tantrums of the toddler, the independence of the teenager, the militancy of pressure groups like OutRage. It is obvious in the jubilation of countries emerging from colonial rule, in the collapse of communism, and in the street parties that accompanied the black vote in South Africa. You have only to suggest there is a place for law in ethics, for colonialism in foreign relations, for male leadership in the family, for censorship in films, to provoke a violent reaction. Freedom is among the most glittering prizes of humankind. It will not be denied. It is the headiest wine in all the world.

CHRISTIANITY AND FREEDOM

What has Christianity to say to this desire for freedom? You might be pardoned for thinking, *Very little,* if you look at the institutional churches. Little sense of freedom in their form of service—it is boringly predictable and unfailingly run from the front. Not much freedom in their behavior patterns—which look very much like a system of do's and don'ts, backed up by heavenly sanctions. In schools and universities the Christian groups are not always notable for their sense of joyous liberation: they sing hymns and keep their noses clean, and who wants to be part of that?

I find it tragic that Christian churches and groups could ever appear in that light. But I have to confess that it is often so. By their economic, social, moralistic, and liturgical conservatism the churches have dismally failed to embody the charter of freedom that is their birthright. For, rightly understood, the Christian life is all about freedom.

Christianity Endorses Freedom

Look at where it all begins, with Abraham, the father of the Jewish race. Here was a man who, at the call of God, ventured out from the settled and familiar into an uncharted future; we read that he "left home, without knowing where he was to go." Central to the Old Testament is the story of the Exodus, when a band of slaves refused to lie down under foreign domination but at the instigation of God, through a revolutionary leader, broke loose from their bondage and set out on a long and perilous journey through trackless desert to the promised land. It was the making of the Jewish people.

Look at the New Testament. At its heart lie a cross and an empty tomb, pointing out the fact that Jesus has pioneered for us a greater freedom than men and women in their wildest dreams had ever imagined possible, a deliverance that included liberation from the consequences and the grip of our failings.

Or look at Christian history. To be sure, there are plenty of shameful episodes, such as the crusades and the Inquisition. We all know about them. They are an excellent stick to beat Christians with, and the church has good cause to be ashamed of its failure to live like its Founder. But who pioneered freedom in education? Who pioneered the right to be cared for in hospitals? Who freed the slaves? Who emancipated women? Who prevented children from working eighteen hours a day in factories? Who fought for racial freedom? Who instituted trade unions? Who brought medicine and education to the developing parts of the world? Who are the freedom fighters in China and Cuba today, just as they were in Eastern Europe during the cold war? In each case you will find courageous Christians who have played a leading part in the fight for freedom.

Reflect on a statement like this: "There is no such thing as Jew and Greek, slave and free, male and female; for you are all one in Christ Jesus" (Gal. 3:28). Where else in classical antiquity do you find a voice like this Christian voice, declaring a manifesto in which all racial, religious, social, and sexual barriers that had divided human beings for centuries had been broken through?

Yes, the Bible is as enthusiastic for freedom as the most revolutionary student or the most dedicated humanist. But it makes a number of important qualifications to the concept.

Is Freedom Possible Without God?

First, Christians would want to maintain that in atheism there is no possibility of finding freedom. That should be evident enough by surveying the track record of all atheistic regimes. But there is a logical reason for it as well. If there is no God, no personal source for this world and human nature, we are left with two sorts of impersonal factors that may govern the universe. And neither of them offers any room for freedom.

The whole world, and ourselves within it, may be totally *determined:* by fate, the stars, or the chemical constituents of our physical makeup. That view underlies the trust in horoscopes, which is a feature in so many magazines these days. It is the creed of behaviorism, advocated by B. F. Skinner and his followers.

However, there is no reason to believe this account of things. If we were totally determined by our chemistry, that would be the end both of freedom and of truth. For even if we were free (which in this view we would not be) to find truth (whatever that might be), we could never *know* whether it was true. Our minds would simply be determined to think that way. There would be no possibility of altering their working. Determinism would govern all.

The alternative atheistic hypothesis would be that the whole world is *random*. Some geneticists are making precisely this claim in the light of microbiology. But does not this view, like determinism, rule out both truth and freedom? If chance is king, there is no truth to be discovered and no freedom to be enjoyed. How could you find truth if your mental processes were random? How could you find freedom in a totally unstructured environment? The modern cult of deconstructionism, which sees truth as merely a statement of our individual preferences or an attempt to hijack others with our claims, is actually the foe not only of truth but also of freedom.

No, on atheistic presuppositions we can have no real freedom. Life is essentially meaningless. However you state the atheistic account of the world, it leads to incoherence. It has no way of explaining how you get personal being in an impersonal world. We derive from time, chance, and the impersonal, do we not? Then how come we cannot treat ourselves and other people as mere collections of atoms? How can we account for shame at murder, for example, or self-sacrifice for a cause? We have immortal longings in our hearts, but there is no eternity to satisfy them. We can pray, but there is no God to listen. We have values, but they are without objective value since from matter we came and to matter we return. Freedom? Certainly not. There is much talk of it in atheistic circles, but it has to be illusory. For in that view, personal being is nothing but a speck of flotsam and jetsam on the ocean of time, space, and the impersonal.

No, if you want freedom, recognize it as the gift of the living God to enable his creatures to share in something of his nature and nobility.

Freedom is not the license to do what you want, but the liberty to do what you ought. And we actually possess a portrait of what that sort of freedom might look like. Needless to say, I am thinking of Jesus. Was there ever a man so free?

The Free Man's Model

He came from a working-class family, yet was as free from inverted snobbery as he was from aggressive ambitiousness. Brought up in a strict Jewish home, he was free from racial and religious prejudices. Raised as a member of a subject race, he was always in control of his circumstances. Strong believer in the Old Testament, he nevertheless felt free to reinterpret its general precepts in individual cases—he was no slave to the system! He never drew a sword, yet his teaching has proved one of the most potent forces for liberation ever since. He never freed a slave or enfranchised a woman, yet his principles have fired the greatest social reforms. He never functioned outside Palestine, yet his gospel has freed men and women and broken down class and color prejudice the world over. He was free to hold on to his life and feather his own nest had he chosen to, yet he voluntarily surrendered his life at the age of about thirty. Why? It was not because the big battalions caught up with him, but because he intended, as he put it, to "give his life as a ransom for many."

Think of Jesus in the courtroom, bound and bleeding from the cat-o'-nine-tails. Was he the prisoner, or were his torturers? Surely they were: prisoners all of jealousy and envy, greed and hate, pride and sadism. But Jesus was free, utterly free.

Think of him before Pilate. He could face the man who had the power of life and death over him and calmly remark, "You could have no power over me unless it had been given you from above." Jesus, not his judge, was truly free.

Think of him at Calvary. The other two crucified with him were cursing, kicking, urinating, as they were nailed to their instruments of torture. Jesus, enduring the same treatment, could pray, "Father forgive them, for they do not know what they are doing." You have to be very free to do that!

Jesus spells freedom. He represents the supreme example of the truly liberated person. All the more reason to listen to him as he gives us his analysis of human bondage. It is utterly radical and unexpected.

Jesus' Analysis of Human Bondage

Jesus is not at all like a modern liberal, ascribing human wickedness to defects in housing, environment, education, or psychological stability. No doubt all these play a part. But he lays his finger on the essential point, one from which we shy away because it is so painfully near the bone. On one occasion he told his Jewish audience,

"If you follow my teaching you will be free." Their reply was prompt—and ludicrous, coming as it did from a subject people: "We were never in bondage to anyone." Jesus' response was devastating: "Whoever does wrong becomes the slave of wrong." On another occasion when his hearers were attributing the cause of defilement to ritual uncleanness, Jesus said,

> Do you not perceive that whatever enters a man from outside cannot defile him? . . . What comes out of a man, that defiles a man. For from within, out of the heart of men, proceed evil thoughts, adulteries, fornications, murders, thefts, covetousness, wickedness, deceit, lewdness, an evil eye, blasphemy, pride, foolishness. All these evil things come from within and defile a man. (Mark 7:18–23 NKJV)

Of course, the insight was not original. It runs through the reflections of honest people down the centuries, though none expressed it so powerfully as Jesus. Herodotus, the father of history, observed, "The greatest sadness in human affairs is this: we aim at so much but fail to achieve it." Seneca, the distinguished Stoic philosopher, admitted, "I am in the grip of habits which fetter me. I cannot escape from the pit I am in unless a higher hand should rescue me." Ovid, the Augustan playboy poet, wryly observed, "I see the better course, and I approve of it: but I follow the worse." Paul, despite his phenomenal emphasis on moral rectitude, had to admit, "The good that I want to do, I cannot do. The evil that I do not want to do, I do." Martin Buber, the Jewish thinker who survived the Holocaust, cried out, "Who can change that intractable thing, human nature? There is a tragedy at the heart of things."

That is the truth. It is true of you and true of me. We are defeated by our own base impulses. We are a walking civil war. A student once wrote forcefully to me, "Why do I need God to control my faults? Should I not strive to better myself? I've tried that for a year now, and succeeded mostly, except during exams when I was bitter and twisted. I've tried to excuse that as abnormal, but I can't. So I'll try harder." Good for her. But it doesn't work. In a later letter she wrote, "I feel so selfish always working and slaving only for myself. Even though I swore in the old days to force myself to become a nicer person, I find I can't. I'm too lazy and I never get round to it."

Choices

The modern cult of freedom is unrealistic, precisely because it does not take account of the perversity of human nature. The humanist is always trying to get around the awkward fact of human sin. The Christian can afford to look it steadily in the face. He knows that we are not simply good at heart. He knows that we are not free to do all we wish because we are in bondage to ourselves. There is something very realistic in the Christian approach to freedom.

What it comes down to is this. Either we can stay free from God and thereby remain in bondage to ourselves, or we can be freed by Christ from the domination of self and gradually become the people we were meant to be, taking our place in the worldwide society of freed people that God is building up. That is the ultimate dimension of freedom, and we all have to make up our minds whether to follow that path or not.

The path to true freedom is rugged and steep. Jesus said, "Whoever wants to hold on to his life will lose it, and whoever is willing to lay his life down will find it." What a paradox! How can it be the case that, as the old prayer had it, "his service is perfect freedom"? The answer is, I suppose, as Bob Dylan's song recognized, "You gotta serve somebody." *Okay,* you may think, *but why should I consider handing over my freedom to Jesus?*

CUTTING THE CHAINS

Let's recap. Our freedom is limited in three ways at least. First, by the rope of wrongdoing that we have woven for ourselves in the past and by which we are bound. Second, by the innate selfishness that constrains us to turn liberty into license. And third, by the fact that we are going to die. The past—spoiled. The present—weak. The future—uncertain. That is the human situation, is it not? It was to remedy this that Jesus the Liberator came.

How Can Jesus Deal with Our Past?

The answer to this question lies in the Cross. There Jesus took responsibility for our failures, and in so doing he removed the barricade that kept us out of touch with God. Do you feel out of touch? Quite right, you are! People have always felt like that. More than 2,500 years ago some of them came to Isaiah and told him so. The answer was straight to the point: "The Lord's hand is not shortened so that it cannot save. His ear is not deaf so that it cannot hear. But your wrongdoings have separated you and your God, and your evil deeds have hid his face from you, so that he does not hear" (Isa. 59:1–2). Our sins erected a sort of soundproof wall between us and God, which our occasional prayers could not pierce. Jesus brought that wall tumbling down at Calvary—it fell on him. He did it to enable us to find access to God instead of a blank wall.

Objections crowd in. How was it fair of God to pun-ish the wrong person in our place? That is not what happened at all. It was not as if God (one party) pun-ished Jesus (another party) for us (a third party). That would have been grossly unjust, and God, as Ruler and Judge of the whole earth, must do what is right. No, the atonement, as we call it, is indeed an at-one-ment because in Christ crucified God and humanity meet. That is where reconciliation takes place. When Jesus died on the cross, he died as a representative human, taking humanity's proper place—the place of being in the wrong, of alienation, of death. But he was not just a man. He was God. "God was in Christ reconciling the world to himself, not counting their sins against them." So far from punishing some third party for the sins of the world (the Bible never says the Father *punished* Jesus), God himself came among us and took the burden of unforgiven sin off our aching shoulders. On the cross he entered into our estrangement; he accepted and absorbed the poison of our guilt. And he did it because he loved us.

You cannot understand it all? Take heart. Nobody can. The encouraging thing is that we don't have to understand it in order to profit by it. I don't understand electricity, but that does not stop me from switching on the light! Of course, I don't deserve to be accepted by God, with no charge against my name. Of course, I can't earn it. I take it as a gift from the loving hand of God, or I do not get it at all. As Archbishop Temple put it, "I can contribute nothing to my own salvation except the sin from which I need to be delivered." We can be set free from the weight of our past failures only through the cross of Christ.

How Can Jesus Make a Difference in Daily Life?

How can he bring freedom there? The answer lies in the Holy Spirit. When Jesus died, that was not the end of him. Not by a long shot. He rose to life again on the third day: we celebrate it at Easter and indeed every Sunday (the day that marks his resurrection). His friends found, to their amazement, that he was liberator not only from sin but also from death. He had risen victorious over it. And when his work here was finished, and he left them to rejoin his Father in heaven, he gave them an amazing gift. It was his Holy Spirit to live inside them. The God who had been *over* them as Father, *alongside* them in Jesus, was now available to live *in* them through the Spirit. Jesus had told them, "It is for your good that I am leaving you. If I do not go, the Spirit will not come, whereas if I go I will send him to you," and again, "I will not leave you bereft. I am coming back to you." The Holy Spirit is the divine gift to make Jesus real to us; that's the heart of the matter.

Such a claim borders on the fantastic. It is like supposing the spirit of Handel or Elvis could come and indwell your personality, enabling you to reflect something of his genius. Of course, that cannot happen. But when God Almighty offers to come and share his life with you, who is to say that is impossible? It is not impossible, as millions of Christians will tell you, because it has happened to them. The only way to be sure is to try it for yourself.

That is the answer God gives to our besetting failure to live up to our own standards, let alone his. He will come and empower us if we ask him. He will fight for us and in us. And make no mistake; it is a fight. God does not overwhelm our free decisions day by day by forcing us to be good. Actually we are just as weak as before we entrusted our lives to him. The only difference is that the mighty Spirit of God is on board now. We can draw on his strength—if we so choose. The sole new factor in the war against evil is the presence of the Holy Spirit in our lives. We can turn to him and ask his help when temptation strikes, or we can battle along on our own and get beaten, just as we always did. But let's be clear on this. The Holy Spirit is God's answer to the moral defeat that spoils our freedom.

What Does Christ Offer for the Future?

The answer to this is the Resurrection. No matter how stoic people seem to be about death while it is remote, it is a very different matter when death strikes. When a close relation dies, there are few indeed who can pretend they do not believe in some sort of continued existence. However shadowy their conception of an afterlife, there has never in human history been a generation of people who did not cherish the hope of liberation from the last enemy. The current fads are reincarnation and near death experiences. In the former you are supposed to work your passage through a variety of existences until eventually you arrive at *nirvana* (i.e., nothingness or nonsensation). Not too exciting either as a destination or as a path to travel, is it? Who wants to soldier through an almost endless succession of lives, maybe as a slave or a rat, in order to qualify for extinction? Definitely not a prospect to shout about.

Near death experiences are very much the rage at present. Sometimes people who have been brought back from the edge of death speak of a dark tunnel and bright light; sometimes they speak of indescribable horror. Not too far away from the biblical teaching of heaven and hell, I should have thought. However, there is only one way we could be sure. That is if someone genuinely came back from the cold.

Someone *has* come back from the cold. His name is Jesus. It happened at the first Easter. No near death experience for him. He was very dead for three days. And he came back, uniquely qualified to inform us about death and what follows. He had told his followers that in his Father's home there were many resting places. He had told them that his death would prepare a place for them. He had told them that where he was going they would all meet. There would be a "festival of friends." But could he be trusted? The Resurrection gives the answer. He can be trusted. He did not just teach about life after death. He rose to new life from under the scythe of the grim reaper. That's something nobody else has ever done. It gives him considerable credibility!

Choose Freedom

In the Middle Ages there was much speculation about whether there was any land in the western Atlantic. Some thought one thing and some another. But after 1492 the matter was no longer in dispute. Christopher Columbus had reached America and returned. From then on he was uniquely qualified to tell people about the land beyond the sea and to guide them there. He was the living proof that there was such a land. He was also the pilot who could take others where he had gone. It is rather like that with the resurrection of Jesus. It not only shows that there is indeed life after death. It also qualifies him to take others there. God has, as the apostle Peter discovered, given us new birth "to a living hope through the resurrection of Jesus Christ from the dead" (1 Peter 1:3). It is mighty good news. It is sheer liberation from the unrelieved gloom that usually settles on us when a loved one dies and also from the chilling grip of terror as we face the last enemy for ourselves.

If you are looking for liberation at the deepest level, you must take death into account. You would be a fool to neglect it because we all have to die. Is your philosophy of freedom big enough to embrace the whole of life, including death?

It is interesting to contrast the characteristic ways in which free thinkers and Christians tend to approach death. Voltaire, for instance, was a lifelong rationalist. Yet he died crying, "O God, save me. Jesus Christ have mercy on me." Some die with great bitterness of spirit. Dylan Thomas, as we have seen, expressed it powerfully, "Do not go gentle into that good night, / Old age should burn and rage at close of day; / Rage, rage against the dying of the light." But however much we rage, it will do no good. Others shrug their shoulders, like Aeschylus long ago, "When the dust drinks up a man's blood, their is no resurrection." At best they can say with the philosopher Thomas Hobbes, "When I die the worms will devour my body, and I will commit myself to the great 'Perhaps.'"

Contrast those statements with the characteristic approach Christians make to death. The radiant courage of martyrs down the ages, the quiet confidence of so many ordinary Christians as they draw near to death, gives substance to Paul's confident claim, "To me to live is Christ and to die is gain." He longed to "depart and to be with Christ which is far better." And he sealed his testimony with his blood.

Such is the freedom Jesus offers. It is a freedom that is big enough to embrace past, present, and future. It is a freedom that gradually liberates us from the self-centeredness that is so corrosive and so destructive of community. It sets us free to serve one another without calculating what we are going to get out of it. It is a freedom that enables us to live a life neither by the rule book nor by hedonistic selfishness, but a life of joyful company with the Christ whose Spirit lives in us and whose service really is perfect freedom. There is no more legalism about it than there is between bride and bridegroom who love each other dearly, and because of that love will do anything to please the other.

There is a price tag to this quality sort of freedom. The cost of letting Christ free you from all you know to be wrong. The cost of allowing him to progressively free you from the grip of self-centeredness. The cost of getting stuck into his family and actively involved in his cause, renouncing the spectator mentality and the wimp-ishness that is terrified to admit whose you are and whom you serve. You have to choose. *You gotta serve somebody.* Who shall it be?

9

Love

THE MODERN MISUNDERSTANDING
OF LOVE

IF EVER THERE WAS A SOCIETY IN TOTAL CONFUSION about love and sexuality, it is ours. Love is undoubtedly our number one interest, but we are not at all sure what it is. We used to think we would find it between our parents. But they are too busy to have time for us, and increasingly they are divorcing. We used to locate it in happy families, but they seem to be almost a thing of the past. We used to look for it in friendship, but these days friendship without sexuality is considered an aberration. A man can hardly have another man over for a cup of coffee in private without being denounced as a homosexual. Even academic interviews are usually conducted with the door open for fear of accusations of sexual harassment. You cannot leave your children in the care of a baby-sitter without the nagging fear that they might be sexually abused. Something has gone seriously wrong. That is obvious. "One sentence will suffice for modern man," said Albert Camus. "He fornicated and he read the newspapers."

Erosion of Morality

Camus put his finger on an important part of the problem. There has been such an erosion of general morality during the past half century that love in the full-blooded sense—embracing not only sexuality but also a sense of partnership, companionship, fidelity, trust, self-giving, respect, and consistency—has almost vanished. Instead selfishness has replaced altruism, hedonism has replaced self-sacrifice, and instant sexual gratification has replaced long-term commitment. No wonder Dudley Moore complains, "I am always looking for meaningful one-night stands." They don't exist.

Malcolm Muggeridge came to see that "sex is the mysticism of materialism, and the only possible religion in a materialistic society." Increasingly, as we saw in a previous chapter, we have been making material success and prosperity our supreme goal, our god. This has all manner of disastrous results, particularly when it is allied to the philosophy of the me generation. Aspects of ourselves, such as worship, adoration, self-giving, tenderness, feelings, are generally banished from the workplace, but they surface in personal relationships, ideally in sexual intercourse.

Since God is out of fashion, it is hardly surprising that sex appears to be the highest good. Sex, so we are told in seemingly every movie, every commercial, every book, every magazine, every billboard, is the greatest goal in life. If you aren't having it, you are hopelessly out of date; you haven't lived. The scandal of premarital sex has disappeared; it is replaced by the scandal of virginity. "There are three really important things in my life," quipped Woody Allen. "The first is sex. Somehow the other two don't seem very important now."

We all know the dangers: a massive rise in teenage pregnancies, sexually transmitted diseases, broken hearts, lies, shattered families, AIDS, and the rest. It makes no difference. We blindly rush ahead following our hormones. Michael Douglas confessed to a group therapy session, "Sex is a wave that just sweeps over me—the impulse, that is. It's compulsive, overpowering. And when the urge comes, I'm helpless every time. I've run the most incredible risks."

Broken Homes

Why do we run these risks? Is it simply because we are following through the sexual revolution of the sixties? That is part of it. The twenty-year-olds of today are the children of the first generation on the pill, the first generation to make personal satisfaction and instant gratification their ultimate concerns. They have never known any other models. But they have been severely damaged by this cult of pleasure and material prosperity in their parents' lifestyle. Selfishness is the name of the game, and selfishness has resulted in the breakdown of the family on a massive scale. The diminishing of mutual commitment is a major element in British and American societies these days. The parents break up because they do not have the moral guts to stick with their vows when things get difficult. But the ones who suffer are the kids. In survey after survey the children of divorce confess their deep longings for an intact family.

The following description is poignant and characteristic:

At night Jean would crawl into her mother's bed and keep her awake as she thrashed around in her nightmares. Andy came home from school with drawings of his mother, his sister and himself clutching each other tightly, their faces forlorn. When they came back from visiting their father, Karen would hear her son in the bathroom throwing up.

The British government's chief medical officer, Dr. Kenneth Calman, has recently highlighted the corrosive legacy of Great Britain's rising divorce rate. It is the highest in Europe, and it is increasing all the time. He outlines some of the consequences for the children. Girls who become part of a stepfamily by the age of sixteen run twice the risk of becoming teenage mothers. Girls under sixteen are three times more likely to leave home because of disagreements or ill feeling, and four times more likely to enter into an early and disastrous marriage than those who continue to live with both parents. Boys have no role model of how a husband and father should behave. And children whose parents have divorced are twice as likely to leave school at sixteen as those from intact families. We are not surprised to hear that the number of people who smoke remains high and drinking and drug use are massively on the increase. Alcohol is involved in 45 percent of fatal automobile accidents involving young people, and 75 percent of all crime is considered to be alcohol related.

Survivors

It is not hard to see where all this has led. It has produced a generation of young adults who are survivors. They have survived the threat of abortion to get into this world in the first place. They have survived abuse and neglect, and the parental selfishness that has either bought them off with presents instead of relationship or given the impression they do not matter by neglect or divorce. They have survived materialist indoctrination through endless hours in front of the TV. They have survived, in many cases, the corruption of the gangs and the streets. They have become very distrustful of people and institutions. They have learned to depend on themselves—they have had to. And yet they have survived. It is immensely impressive.

"Spiritually starved, economically traumatized, educationally deprived, condemned to a bleak economic future and robbed of the hope that should characterize youth," as William Mahedy succinctly puts it, they are amazing. And two things have burned deeply into their souls. They know that the material things that bewitched their parents will never satisfy. And despite their initial and thoroughly understandable distrust, they have a deep longing for profound relationships. In an age when there is a desperate shortage of role models, has Jesus Christ anything significant to say on this most crucial of all issues? Is Christianity able to help our confusions over love?

THE CHRISTIAN UNDERSTANDING OF LOVE

The basic assumption of Christianity is the precise opposite of the hypothesis advanced by Sigmund Freud. He
thought that the idea of a loving God sprang from human
love. We thus project our father image into the sky, call
it God, and apply the same emotions to it as we do to
our own fathers. So human love is primary and real;
love for God is derived and illusory. Christianity, on the
contrary, asserts that God's love is primary, and that all
human love derives from it and is in some measure (however distorted) a pale reflection of God's love, the love
that makes the world go round.

Far from being the projection of the parent image
into the empty sky, love is the most powerful force in
the world precisely because it reflects the fundamental
reality about the universe. It comes from God. And God
is love. We love because he first loved us. That is the fundamental Christian conviction on the subject. Love, if
you like, is another of God's footprints in the sand of
our lives (see Chapter 1), to point us toward him and
drive us into his arms. Let's try this hypothesis for size.
We shall find seven things in God's love that are mir-
rored by the best in human love, seven elements that
will give us a grip on this slippery concept of love.

1. Love Is Personal

You cannot have love in a vacuum. The very word involves relationship between persons. To say "I love" is meaningless. To say "I love you" is great. And that is what the whole New Testament maintains: "God so loved the world . . . the Son of God loved me." This means that I am the object of his love. You may not feel that way. You may think, *God could love everyone else maybe, but he could not love me.* Well, Jesus came to show that God does love every one of us. His life is the window through which the love of God shines through to us.

How else could God possibly show he cares, except in terms of a human life? A life spent for others, a life poured out in selfless giving. Jesus showed us what God is like. He revealed as much of the Father's love as we can possibly take in. Rightly he claimed, "He who has seen me has seen the Father."

It comes down to this. You and I don't have to look for God. God is looking for us. He faces us with the person of Jesus and says, in effect, "There, that is love. Utter self-giving to the utterly undeserving. Will you have it or not?" The love that spun the universe into space has erupted in Jesus. Love confronts us in person and looks for a response. The crucial issue is, "What do you make of Jesus?" not "Does God exist?" That is the wrong way to formulate the question. It leaves comfortable room for argument and evasion. But the living God is no "it" to be analyzed and argued about. God is the supreme "I" to be encountered. And encounter us he does in the person of Jesus—not as a proposition to be argued about but as a person to be met. You cannot love a proposition. You cannot argue about a person. The only way to find out for sure is by meeting. All human love is, by its very nature, interpersonal. God's love cannot be less.

2. Love Is Satisfying

You know how it is when two people fall in love. They are utterly taken up with each other, deeply satisfied. They have begun to taste a new and shared life, and it is wonderful. "When someone really loves you, that's when your life begins."

Unfortunately it often dies very quickly; sometimes it ripens into marriage. But even so, all human love is incomplete. It points to something beyond itself. It reaches out toward an experience that it does not itself satisfy. Hardly surprising, if the Great Lover is excluded from our lives. Oh, I know we don't picture him as that. He feels like the Great Policeman. His aim, we fear, is to make life respectable and dull, not joyful and satisfying. Well, wherever we got that idea from, it owes nothing to the New Testament or the person of Jesus, who brought joy with him wherever he went. "I have come that you may have life, life in all its fullness," said Jesus. Those who entrust their lives to him know the truth of that claim. Francis Thompson's classic poem "The Hound of Heaven" describes his efforts to keep God out of his life because he thought God would spoil, not satisfy. He eventually found out his mistake. The heavenly Pursuer cries out, "Thou dravest love from thee, who dravest Me."

One of the most striking characteristics of modern society is fear. Often disguised, it is always there. Fear of loneliness, of unemployment, of betrayal, of failure, of ridicule, of death. Bertrand Russell, in his book *Why I Am Not a Christian,* says this of Christianity: "Religion is based mainly on fear . . . fear of the mysterious, fear of defeat, fear of death. Fear is the basis of the whole thing." He goes on, "Science can help us to get over this craven fear in which mankind has lived so long." How ironic! Science has plunged us into a morass of fear, fear even for the continued existence of our planet. To be sure, some religions, notably animism, are based on fear, but faith in Jesus could never be described as that. "There is no fear in love; perfect love banishes fear. . . . Anyone who is afraid has not attained to love in its perfection," wrote one of Jesus' closest friends (1 John 4:18).

Real Christianity releases us from fear, as Christ's love pours in. My fear about my inadequacy is banished by a love that accepts me just as I am. My sense of loneliness in this mechanical and impersonal world is met by the constant companionship of the risen Jesus. He lives! He is available—all the time.

Do you want a really satisfying life? The big three— money, sex, and power—will not do it. They will not satisfy the deepest cravings of your heart. But if you allow the love of God to enter you and work through you to others, you will begin a difficult life but a profoundly satisfying one. You'll be doing what you were made for.

3. Love Is Searching

They say love is blind. They are talking nonsense. A person is never so much awake as when in love. Love searches the loved one, wants to find out every trait of character, every mood, every response. Lovers cannot tolerate any subterfuge, any secrets. They want to know the object of their affection through and through.

God is just as searching in his love. He cannot be deceived or kept at arm's length. His eyes are like a laser beam. What does he see as he looks at you and me?

Well, to be sure, he sees *spoiled* lives. In an age when humankind is thought once more to be the measure of all things (as if that doctrine had not proved disastrous in the ancient world, the Renaissance, and the Enlightenment), the main trouble is people themselves. It was G. K. Chesterton who wrote the shortest letter to the *Times* on record. The subject was "What's wrong with the world?" and Chesterton replied, "Sir, I am." Greed, lust, hate, dishonesty, callousness, jealousy—the seeds of these things lie buried in all of us. We were born with them, as were our forebears. And we cannot eradicate them, try as we may. Our disease is endemic. As Professor Herbert Butterfield observed in his book *Christianity and History,* "It is essential not to have faith in human nature. Such a delusion is a very modern one and very disastrous. History uncovers man's universal sin." When the mask of decency is torn off our respectable faces, God sees us in our true colors. But that is not all.

God sees not only spoiled but *selfish* lives. The apostle John put it like this: "Not that we loved God, but that he loved us." Certainly we do not love God. We barely tolerate him. Tennyson was way off the mark when he said, "We needs must love the highest when we see it." When the highest came, we nailed him to a cross. He proved too uncomfortable, too bright a light. This is our condemnation: "Men loved darkness rather than light because their deeds were evil" (John 3:19).

Despite all the Father's lavish provision for us, we have, like the prodigal son, gone off, turned our backs on home, and deliberately chosen to live in a far country. We find out, sooner or later, what a miserable place it is. In the meantime, our self-centeredness breaks his heart.

4. Love Is Lasting

One of the most terrible things in life is to have love removed. To be dropped, to be jettisoned by the one we love, is nearly unbearable. Many of us know that the love of our parents is not lasting. They get bored with us, or they divorce. They do not seem to care deeply enough to stay around. But we had hoped for better things in our own love life. Sadly it often does not happen. "All that's important is that she used to love you and now she doesn't," wrote Andrew Davies in *Getting Hurt*. "You're losing her, it's over, and it hurts. You felt from the start she could do you harm, and now you know for certain. . . . You've lost her. You're the unseated rider. You're the wounded soldier. You hurt. . . . Will it last for ever, feeling like this? I don't know."

D. H. Lawrence, one of the most sensitive writers on love, asked himself in *Women in Love* what would happen if the human race ran into a cul-de-sac and destroyed itself. His hope was that the timeless creative mystery would bring forth a new race to carry on the game. That's the best a sensitive agnostic can suppose. But that is not the way of the God who is love. He does not abandon us when we blow it comprehensively. He calls to us, pleads with us, comes to find us, dies for us. He assures us that his love is endless. Nothing in all creation will be able to tear us from his arms. He will never leave us nor forsake us. He will not divorce us, cast us away. Unlike any human lover, the Lord stays with us through thick and thin. And in so doing he satisfies our deepest longings for unending relationship, the longing he has himself implanted within us. Human love goes a long way, but not far enough. God's love goes the whole hog.

5. Love Is Sacrificial

We never know how much others love us until we see how much they are willing to sacrifice and suffer for us. The sacrificial element is the yardstick of true love. So much that passes for love today knows nothing of this costly, sacrificial element. It is, in fact, not love at all, but thinly disguised lust. Lust says "I." Love says "You." Lust grasps. Love gives. Lust wants to enjoy. Love is willing to sacrifice. Perhaps this lack of true love in many people these days makes it more difficult for them to appreciate the love of God, for that is all give and no take. He gave himself to this awful world we had so messed up. He gave himself to the toughest of physical and economic conditions. He gave himself to abuse and rejection. He gave himself to the most terrible death anyone can die. We know it so well that it has lost its power to grip us. Perhaps a human example may help.

The story is told in Ernest Gordon's *The Miracle on the River Kwai* of a prisoner of war camp in World War II. The morale of the allied prisoners was very low as they slaved on the Burma Railway for their captors. So low that the men forgot all common decencies and descended to the level of animals in order to survive. It was everyone for himself.

One day after work a count was taken of the tools, as usual. There was one short. So all the men were lined up and questioned about the lost tool. The man who had taken it was ordered to step from the ranks. Nobody moved. The officer in charge became livid with fury. He raved at the prisoners and threatened to shoot all of them if the guilty party did not own up. It was obvious that he meant what he said. Suddenly, deliberately, one man stepped forward. He was immediately clubbed to death by the Japanese.

The squad was marched back to the camp, and the tools were checked through again. It was discovered that a mistake had been made at the first count: *they were all there!* The incident made a profound impression on the whole camp. It revolutionized their morale. Here was a man who was completely innocent, but he had died a voluntary death in order to save his doomed comrades. It was self-sacrifice out of the normal run; it was fantastic.

It is something like that with the love of God. Humankind is doomed, like the men in that squad—with the difference that we all stand justly condemned. And such were his love and self-sacrifice that Jesus willingly stepped forward and took our place so that we could all go free. He deliberately undertook our doom so that we might live. God loves like that! He "sent his Son to be the Savior of the world." And we can be quite sure that we are accepted because of what he has done for us, although in ourselves we are quite unacceptable. Such is the fruit of Love's self-sacrifice.

6. Love Is Challenging

When a girl loves a boy with a deep, unselfish love, when she is prepared to sacrifice all for him, particularly if the boy feels that the girl is far too good for him, then he is challenged to the very roots of his being. He knows he cannot simply trifle with a love like that. He must do something about it. It demands self-giving in response.

Nothing less will do. He must make up his mind whether he is going to commit himself to the girl or walk away. There is no other option.

So it is with the love God offers us. It challenges us to decide. Remember *God* loves you like this. The God who made the world and all that is in it. The God who is personal. The God who offers you his Holy Spirit to enter, strengthen, and enhance your personality. The God who knows you through and through because he made you, and yet who loves you so much that he laid down his life for you. It was the personal challenge of this love that the apostle Paul could not find it in him to refuse. "The Son of God loved *me*," he cried, "and gave himself for *me*" (Gal. 2:20).

What will you do with this love of God? Is it not time to decide? Perhaps you have been keeping him at arm's length? Perhaps you have been deliberately rebelling against him, maybe for years? Will you continue to grieve him by refusing his loving pardon and remaining at loggerheads with him? Or do you want the love of God to come flooding into your life and flow through you to others? Do you want him to come in and clean you up? He won't do anything until you ask him. For love never forces itself upon us. Love waits. Love woos. I shall say more about response in the final chapter, but notice one thing more about love. It is equally true of human love and of divine love.

7. *Love Is Infectious*

History is full of stories telling how persistent love eventually managed to break through and the loved one responded. Their union often results in a loving family atmosphere that powerfully affects all visitors to the home. Well, God's love is like that too. Once we have welcomed it on board—and not before—it begins to become infectious.

You see it in a man like President Mandela. He surrendered to the love of God while he was a prisoner on Robben Island, so I am told. The results are plain for all to see. No bitterness, though he might so easily have harbored it. Nothing but a warmth that is recognized the world over and is doing a great deal to heal the hurts of South African society. You see it in a man like Chuck Colson, who used to be Richard Nixon's hatchet man, with an office next to the president's in the White House. He was disgraced and imprisoned through his complicity in the Watergate scandal, yet his whole life and subsequent career have been transformed since he responded to the love of God. The Lord did not give up on this proud lawyer but pursued him gently until he gave in. The result? Since his release, he has devoted his life to founding and extending worldwide an organization called Prison Fellowship. It is designed to bring to prisoners everywhere the good news of God's love that has made a new man of him. Colson would be the first to tell you that we can't pour out love until it has been poured in.

And that brings us back to where we began, with human relationships and sexual love. For once we have allowed God to pour into our hearts his satisfying, lasting, sacrificial love, it will extend to all our relationships, including our friends and our spouses. We shall not find ourselves in bondage to a rule book, nor shall we selfishly do our own thing. There will be less of "I must have" and more of "I give," once we have allowed Christ's love to warm us. There will be a firm refusal to exploit others, to hurt them, to jettison them. There will be a lot less of the instant gratification and a lot more of the long-term self-giving. That is the way to be fully human in our relationships.

It is interesting that many people, especially young people, are beginning to move in this direction. Years ago Marilyn Monroe exclaimed, "A sex symbol becomes a thing. I hate being a thing." So do we all. The American novelist and social critic Ayn Rand put it well in a *Playboy* interview, "I consider promiscuity immoral. Not because sex is evil, but because it is too good and too important." Eric Clapton made the same discovery:

I'm finding out in my recovery that I've always used sex as some kind of tool. As a way of holding someone hostage, to make an impression, fixing myself, fixing them. It's never been what it really is, which is an expression of love and as a means of continuing our existence on earth. But I've found I'm happier if I'm doing it in a monogamous relationship, and there's no deceit, and no lies, and it's a pure expression of affection.

And writer Peter Wilkes is sharper still:

Sex says "I give myself to you," while marriage does the giving. Sex is like a parable of marriage. Marriage is the true self-giving. Within it sex expresses that commitment a couple have publicly made in their vows to each other. Outside of marriage sex is simply a lie. It says "I give myself to you," but denies the reality, for you are not married until you are married.

We all know how difficult it is to go in the direction those quotations are pointing. It is hard, though possible, to say no and to exercise self-discipline. Woody

Allen comes to mind again: "I want to tell you a terrific story about oral contraception. I asked this girl to sleep with me and she said 'No.'"

Many young people today are having the courage to say just that—not because sex is bad but because it is the most precious thing we have. It is not to be soiled. And although members of the generation of eighteen to twenty-fives have been raised in a very permissive atmosphere, they are well aware of the ravages of sexual indiscipline. Although they have been badly burned in their growing years, and have become more street-wise and distrustful of all institutions, they are looking instinctively toward personal relationships that have integrity and deep commitment. That is a true instinct. It meshes very closely with the Christian conviction that love makes the world go round, and that love comes from God, who perfectly embodies it. It is personal, this love, pure, sacrificial, and constant. And it is profoundly fulfilling. I think Jesus would say to lovers like that, "You are not far from the kingdom of God."

But still we have to choose. Shall we make room for this quality of love in our relationships, love that we can get only once we open up to the Great Lover? Or shall we go with the crowd and regard relationships as there to be exploited and sex to be treated as a plaything? I have just seen a television interview with Hugh Hefner, founder and editor of *Playboy* magazine. He personally embodied the *Playboy* philosophy of sex and its lifestyle. He admitted to having slept with more than a thousand girls. If sex is a plaything and means nothing but pleasurable copulation, let's follow Hugh Hefner. If it is a sacrament, and means total self-giving to another, let's follow Jesus Christ. The choice is ours.

10

Choices

I HATE MAKING DECISIONS. BUT UNFORTUNATELY THEY are necessary. And often they determine the future for a long time to come. I remember when my O-level results made me decide between modern languages and classics. There was very little in it. I chose classics for reasons that I suppose must have seemed good at the time. All I know is that my life would have been entirely different had I chosen to go the other path.

While I was at the university, I saw quite a lot of people making an informed decision to follow Jesus Christ; I also saw people deciding not to. It always made a great deal of difference. I recall one man wrestling with the issue as we talked late one night. It was obvious the next morning that he had reached his decision, and that it was to keep well clear of Jesus Christ. I was amazed in the months that followed to see his life disintegrate:

the college took away his scholarship, and his life fell apart. I do not know, of course, whether these things were connected, though I suspect they were. He had made his bed, and he proceeded to lie on it. I have not been able to forget it.

I guess some of you will, if you have persisted thus far with the book, realize that it is time to make up your minds about Jesus of Nazareth. His first recorded words in the Gospels are, "The time has come. God's kingly rule is breaking in. Change direction, and believe the good news." He followed that with a personal challenge: "Come, follow me."

I find it very interesting that Jesus does not come proclaiming the *church*. Important as it is for Christians to meet together, churchgoing alone does not make you a Christian.

Nor does Jesus tell them that they must believe the *creeds*. Israel had a clearly defined creed, but it was very possible, then as now, to make the right noises without personally committing yourself. There is a world of difference between saying, "I believe the Republican Party will win the next election," and "I believe in the Republican Party." Saying the creed does not make you a Christian.

Equally, Jesus does not come proclaiming any *ceremony* of initiation. John the Baptist had done that, but not Jesus. Ceremonies have an important place in all our lives, but they do not by themselves change anything. Christians have an initiation ceremony, baptism. It is very important. But just as a kiss can be a formality rather than an expression of passionate commitment, so can baptism. Baptism alone does not make you a Christian.

Real Christianity is a *companionship* with Jesus Christ. That is what we need to decide about.

CHOOSE THE UPHILL ROAD

Jesus offers us many things that are very attractive. As we have seen more than once in these pages, Jesus embodies the most magnetic *example* for us to try to follow. He is indeed the Light of the World, and we can do no better than to tread in his footsteps.

He offers us *forgiveness* for the dark things in our lives that we hardly dare admit even to ourselves. Nobody else offers that because nobody else has picked up the tab. That is what he did for all of us on the cross. We just need to claim our part in it. And what a relief it is when we do.

Jesus offers us *companionship*. He is the One who conquered death, the man who came back from the cold. Death can never touch him again; he has triumphed over it. So because he is alive, he can always be around to share life with us. What other friend can do that?

Jesus offers us *significance*. So many people these days feel utterly insignificant in the face of the environmental, societal, and economic forces that dwarf us. But God does not regard us that way. He sees us as adopted sons and daughters in his royal family. He sees us as those for whom he was content to die. To him we are all very special. We can walk high.

Jesus offers us *purpose* in life. When we are young, we have all sorts of aims. Some of them we achieve; some of them we don't. But what is the purpose of life itself? The Bible gives us a breathtaking answer. It is to know the living God and enjoy him forever. And we are to become his representatives in a world that on the whole does not want to know. We are called to be his ambassadors, his task force. No small honor.

Jesus offers us *challenge*. We like challenges—to climb a mountain or face an endurance test. But these are comparatively short-lived. Jesus' challenge is lifelong: to come and follow him, day by day, come what may, to the end of our lives. Tough, but worthwhile.

One thing more. Jesus offers us *life beyond the grave*. The only person in the whole of history who broke the death barrier and rose to a new dimension of life on Easter offers to have us to his home once this life is over. Some offer. No wonder wise men and women still follow him.

But there is a cost to everything in life that is worthwhile. And there is a serious cost to the Christian life. One shrewd person put it like this: "The entrance fee to the Christian life is nothing at all—but the annual subscription is all you have got." The cost of our salvation was paid by Christ on the cross, and some people never become his disciples because they are too proud to accept a gift. But once you do respond to Jesus you will find that you are caught up in being his disciple and part of his people.

It will cost you your sins. Jesus calls us to repent, or change direction. That means a fond farewell to all the stuff in our lives that we know is rubbish. It does not mean you will never fall into the muck again; we all do from time to time. But it does mean that you have deliberately changed direction. You cannot rid yourself of your failings. If you could, you would not need Jesus. Jesus can rid you of them, but you have to let him. You cannot have Christ as your Savior and also hold on vigorously to the bad things in your life from which he wants to set you free.

It will cost you your selfishness. We are all pretty keen on our independence. We like to run our lives as we please. And when Jesus meets us, he comes as Lord and Master as well as Savior and Friend. In a word, he's the boss; we are the learners. And that is not easy for us. But it makes sense, does it not? After all, he knows you inside out. He knows what is best for you and where you fit in with his good purposes. So why not put yourself without reserve into his hands? You will often have an argument with him over some issue and want to withdraw some of that initial surrender. But are you willing in principle to say, "Lord, come and take over the whole of my life. I want to be yours"? That is what he longs for. And in that surrender, curiously enough, you will find a freedom you never dreamed of. For you are handing yourself over not to an institution or a rule book, but to Someone who loves you dearly and will never harm you. He is utterly to be trusted. What does not work is a half-hearted Christian life. I've tried it, and it is sheer misery!

It will also cost you your secrecy. How we love to think that our religion is our own affair and that it is something we don't talk about. Well, that is not an option for us if we start taking Jesus seriously. He warned that if we did not acknowledge him before our fellow human beings, he would not acknowledge us before his Father in heaven. He calls us to be candles in the surrounding darkness, salt among the rotting meat, a city set on a hill that cannot be hidden. Jesus always seems to have called people to open decision and discipleship. It is good for us actually. It helps to nail our colors to the mast. Who ever heard of being a soldier and yet ashamed to wear the uniform? Don't think that if you start to follow Jesus, you will be able to keep it quiet. After all, what use to him is a secret disciple? He wants people who will start to change society and be unembarrassed to be known as his followers.

So it is costly to follow him. Make no mistake about it. But it is more costly to say no to his call. Jesus constantly reminded his hearers that they would have to live with the consequences of their decision. In one of his famous parables he invited all and sundry to the banquet of the Christian life, but told us in the same story that the door is shut on those who refuse the invitation. Does that seem a bit hard? Not at all. God makes complete provision for us to come into his presence, forgiven and cleaned up—and all at his expense. If we reject the means he has generously provided, how can we presume on his mercy? If we spit in his eye and spurn his love, we have only ourselves to blame for missing the party. We need to choose.

CHOOSE TO WELCOME JESUS IN

I have mentioned quite often in this book that we need to come to a firm decision whether or not to commit ourselves to Jesus Christ. You may be wondering how on earth you might do it. It is not difficult. You come to him just as you are, without trying to patch yourself up and make yourself good enough. You come at once—procrastination can be the thief not only of time but also of eternity. You come simply and sincerely and tell him that you want to be his follower.

A famous verse in the Bible has helped millions follow Jesus. I love it because it was the thing that brought me to him when I was very confused about how to begin in earnest. It runs like this: "I stand at the door and knock. If anyone hears My voice and opens the door, I will come in to him and dine with him, and he with Me" (Rev. 3:20 NKJV). That is the offer of Jesus himself. It is as if each life is a house. He made that house in the first place. He bought it back when we had stolen it from him. So it is doubly his, but he will never force our hand. He waits for us to respond. And the wonder of it is that he offers to come in and share the house with us if we invite him to do so.

The context is very interesting. Those words were addressed to church people. They lived in a town called Laodicea, which was very prosperous. Probably the church was, too, because the members boasted, "I am rich. I have prospered. I don't need a thing." That's the sort of attitude many modern people have: "Don't hassle me. I'm fine." Well, Jesus told them that they were far from fine. They were "wretched, pitiful, poor, blind and naked." That's how he saw them: pathetically conceited but actually in deep need. And foolishly they kept him, their real provider, out. They had everything in Christianity except the heart of it, a personal relationship with Jesus himself. That was why he told them they needed to change direction and let him in. And he promised that if they asked, he would indeed come in. He would not just pay a courtesy visit; he would stay with them for good. It would not be a miserable time if they asked him on board; it would be like a splendid dinner party.

And the marvelous thing about this promise is that it is no mere figure of speech. When we come in repentance and trust to offer our lives to Jesus Christ, then he does indeed come into us by his unseen presence, which we call the Holy Spirit. That is what makes a person a real Christian. I may have been baptized, and that is important: it is the badge of belonging. I may believe it all in my head. That is important, too, for we need to be clear about what we are doing. But the third and most important strand in becoming a Christian is to invite the Spirit of Jesus to come in and make his home with us. If I have not done that yet, then I am not a Christian in the full sense of the word: "If anyone does not have the Spirit of Christ, he is not His" (Rom. 8:9 NKJV). So said Paul, and he should know!

That is where it all begins. We have to choose whether to welcome Jesus' unseen Holy Spirit into our personalities or not. The choice is ours. It is the most important choice we ever make in the whole of our lives. And if you in humility and gratitude utter a prayer of surrender and welcome to the loving Christ who has been longing for this day, then he will come into your very being, and he promises, "I will never leave you nor forsake you" (Heb. 13:5 NKJV). It is basically very simple. If you will come to him, he will come to you. And there is no possibility he will reject you. "The one who comes to Me I will by no means cast out," he promises (John 6:37 NKJV). So you are safe with him. And you will find that nothing less than a new life has begun, a life where you are in Christ and he is in you. "Therefore, if anyone is in Christ, he is a new creation; old things have passed away; behold, all things have become new" (2 Cor. 5:17 NKJV). That's how you could begin when you feel the time has come for decision.

It may be that you are not quite sure whether or not you have made that commitment and prayed that sort of prayer. Very well, why not do it now, and make sure? Tell him how you feel, in your own words, or if you prefer, pray something like this:

> *Lord Jesus Christ, I realize there is a lot in my life that is wrong and hurts you deeply. I want to turn my back on it. I am not really sure whether I have entrusted my life to you before. But in any case I'm going to firm it up now. I believe you died and rose again so that you could be my Savior and my Lord. Thank you for your wonderful offer to come into my life and never leave me. Here and now, Jesus, I ask you to come in and take up residence in my life today and for always. Please give me the courage and the strength I shall need if I am to follow you properly. Amen.*

You will find that is the best decision you have ever made and probably the hardest too!

CHOOSE TO TRUST HIS PROMISES,
NOT YOUR FEELINGS

When we start following Jesus, we make a great enemy as well as a great friend. The enemy is the devil. You may not believe in him right now. No matter, you will soon discover his power. He is far from pleased that you have taken a stand for Jesus Christ. If he can't get you back, he will do his level best to make you fall.

The first assault will almost certainly be doubt. *How could I be sure he has accepted me? What if I don't feel any different?* Take heart. Almost everyone has these early doubts. They are typical. But it is most important to learn how to handle them.

If we rely on feelings alone, we shall be in serious trouble. It is unlikely that we shall feel very aware of Christ when we have a high temperature or a splitting headache. But facts are not altered by feelings—though our enjoyment of them is! And the facts are plain.

First, God the Father gives us his word that he welcomes into his own family all who accept Jesus for themselves. Listen: "As many as received Him . . . He gave the right to become children of God" (John 1:12 NKJV). God does not break his promises. Have you received him? Then you *are* in the family.

Second, let's get some clarity on this matter of evil, or "sin" as Christians often call it. The New Testament uses three main words for it in the original Greek, which can be translated as "shortcoming," "offense," and "rebellion." We have come short of God's standards. We have broken his laws. We are rebels against his love. That inevitably puts us in the wrong with him. It makes us guilty. But when we entrusted ourselves to Jesus, things began to change. It takes a long time to grow like Jesus, but the guilt is dealt with at once.

On the cross Jesus paid our debts in full, though it cost him hell. He pressed the delete key, and our sins were wiped away. But it is a favorite ploy of the enemy to remind us of past failures and tell us what a disaster we are. "What, you a Christian? Don't kid yourself. There, you have done it again." That sort of attack is very dispiriting until we learn to face the enemy with the objective *fact* of Christ's death. Tell him you know that you are a disaster, but that Christ "carried away your sins in his own body on the cross" and the job never needs to be repeated. Tell the tempter to get lost. He will soon give up tempting you to doubt that you are a Christian. He has plenty of other ploys!

Third, the Holy Spirit has been given us, and God does not revoke his gifts. It is the Spirit's job to assure us we belong: "The Spirit Himself bears witness with our spirit that we are children of God, and if children, then heirs—heirs of God and joint heirs with Christ" (Rom. 8:16–17 NKJV).

This sounds good, but how does the Spirit make his presence felt? There are a number of ways, and the apostle John told us about them in his first letter.

There's a new sense of pardon. A wonderful sense that we are clean. "If anyone sins, we have an Advocate with the Father, Jesus Christ the righteous. And He Himself is the propitiation for our sins" (1 John 2:1–2 NKJV).

There's a new desire to please God. Previously I did not care whether I pleased him or not. But now I care very much. I don't want to hurt the One I love. That is an evidence of inner change. "By this we know that we are in Him. He who says he abides in Him ought himself also to walk just as He walked" (1 John 2:5–6 NKJV).

There's a new attitude toward other people. "Whoever does not practice righteousness is not of God, nor is he who does not love his brother." Again, "Whoever has this world's goods, and sees his brother in need, and shuts up his heart from him, how does the love of God abide in him?" (1 John 3:10, 17 NKJV).

There's a new appreciation of Christian companionship. "We know that we have passed from death to life, because we love the brethren" (1 John 3:14 NKJV). John was speaking of fellow Christians. They may have seemed a strange bunch previously, but once we have responded to Christ's call, we begin to find ourselves actually wanting to be with them, to learn from them, and to encourage one another. Birds of a feather flock together.

There's a new power over evil. "Whoever abides in Him does not sin." How is this possible? Because "He who is in you is greater than he who is in the world" (1 John 3:6; 4:4 NKJV). This is where the other side of God's handling of evil comes in. He broke the back of it and paid the penalty for it once for all on the cross. But he gradually releases us from the power of evil through his unseen revolutionary force, which Christians call the Holy Spirit. For once we have said yes to Christ, the Holy Spirit enters our lives and becomes a permanent resident. He is stronger than the forces of evil to which we are so prone. And he will give us the strength to overcome if we cry out to him for help when temptation strikes.

There's a new joy and confidence. Needless to say Christians have to go through periods of pain and sadness like everyone else. But there is an underlying joy even then. It comes from fellowship with the Lord and support from his people. The apostle alluded to it in the first few verses of his letter: "We write to you that your joy may be full" (1 John 1:4 NKJV).

There's a new experience of answered prayer. We probably prayed previously (most people do) but were never quite sure that the prayer had gotten through. But once we are linked with the Jesus who died and rose again, the sound barrier of sin and alienation that blocked us from God and made us feel we were praying to ourselves has been pierced. Prayer will gradually become companionship with God. We shall delight to share things with him, and the answers will begin to come. "This is the assurance we have in approaching God: that if we ask anything according to his will he hears us, and if we know that he hears us—whatever we ask—we know that we have what we asked of him" (1 John 5:14–15). We do not always get what we ask for, of course. But we do have the assurance of being heard. God will answer as he sees fit.

John summed it up in a delightful way. He said in effect, "He who believes in the Son of God has the witness in himself; he who does not believe God has made Him a liar." And this is God's solemn word: "God has given us eternal life, and this life is in His Son. He who has the Son has life; he who does not have the Son of God does not have life" (1 John 5:10–12 NKJV). Isn't that delightfully clear? Whether or not you have spiritual life depends on whether or not you have responded to the invitation of Jesus to share your life with him. If you have him and he has you, then you *have* eternal life. Not *will have* when you die; you have it already. God guarantees it. For his eternal life is all wrapped up in Jesus. If you have Jesus, you already have begun to taste a life with God that will last forever. Not surprisingly, therefore, John concluded, "These things I have written to you who believe in the name of the Son of God, that you may know that you have eternal life" (1 John 5:13 NKJV).

You and I have a choice then: whether to rely on our own volatile and changeable feelings about our status as Christians or take God at his word. The latter is the way to assurance. And unless we are sure we belong, we stand very little chance of growing in the Christian life.

CHOOSE TO GROW

It is sad to see someone who has never grown; whether physically or mentally. Unfortunately in the Christian family there are many who have never grown. They have begun their walk with Christ, but they have not continued to give it priority, and so they have not developed into Christian maturity. You see, we can choose. There is no compulsion about it after we become Christians any more than there was before.

God offers us many means of growth. There is a vast amount of literature on the subject. I can give it only headline treatment now.

He offers us a certificate. A certificate to show we belong. Baptism is the Christian certificate of membership. There's the inner side of belonging when we entrust our lives to Christ. But that needs to be matched by the outer side when we show the world that we are not ashamed to be disciples of Christ. If you have secretly committed your life to Christ, you need to ensure that you have been publicly baptized. Baptism is like the adoption papers of some impoverished child when welcomed into a loving family. It is like the certificate of citizenship that most countries use. It is like the contract you normally find in any employment. You see, it has two sides. It is the pledge of all God is offering to us, on the one hand. And on the other, it is the pledge of our grateful and wholehearted response.

We need this tangible sign of belonging. It is an important part of being a Christian. It would be easy on a bad day to doubt whether we really meant it when we asked Christ into our lives. Was our faith strong enough? Well, that is where baptism comes in—to assure us that we belong.

A young bride might find herself wondering drowsily in her half-sleep whether she really was married or had just been dreaming. She has only to feel her wedding ring to be sure. Baptism is that wedding ring.

A Canadian crossing into the States will be questioned about his citizenship. He has only to show his card for the matter to be settled. Baptism is that certificate of citizenship.

An adopted child may well wonder at times whether she belongs. The adoption certificate settles the matter. Baptism is that adoption certificate.

That is why baptism is so important. It is not just meant to be a sign to other people that we are Christians; it is meant to be a source of firm assurance to us.

If you haven't been baptized already, it is time to get the matter sorted out.

He offers us a map. The map is the Bible. It is a detailed and very descriptive map of how we can progress in our lives until finally we meet the Lord in heaven. It is a very comprehensive guide with promises to claim, examples to follow, warnings to heed, prayers to use. Above all it brings us face-to-face with the Lord himself. He inspired this book. He reveals not just his will but also himself in its pages. There is a lovely saying of Martin Luther's about the reason for Bible reading: "As we come to the cradle in order to find the baby, so we come to the Scriptures in order to find the Christ." Sometimes we will find it almost a talking book as some bit comes alive and strikes us forcibly. Sometimes we will find it more of a picture gallery as we see what God did in other lives in the past and learn from that. Sometimes it will be a torch to help us along a particularly dark part of the route. Sometimes it will be a fire to warm us, sometimes a hammer to break down our proud independence. Sometimes it will be a meal to feed us spiritually, and sometimes a mirror to see what we look like—and then take the appropriate action! One thing stands out clearly in Christian history the world over. Feed on this book and you will grow. Neglect it and you will remain small spiritually. We have to choose.

He offers us a meal. I am so thankful that Jesus did not leave behind him some imposing ecclesiastical institution. He left a meal for us to remember him by and to meet him in. What could be more delightful than that? It is a very special meal. For like the Jewish Passover meal that it replaced for the followers of Jesus, it had a number of different aspects to it.

In the Communion meal I look *back* to the Cross with gratitude, and my love is renewed as I reflect on his sacrifice.

I look *into* my own soul and see the areas that need attention—and then I can open them to him for treatment.

I look *up* to the risen Jesus and claim his presence, which brings such joy to the heart and strength on the way.

I look *forward* to heaven, the final banquet when this world is over—and I praise him for his provision for me even beyond the cold river of death.

And then I look *out* on the needy world, hungry for the meal he offers, though usually unaware of that hunger. And I know I am being recommissioned for service.

Now all this is not an individual matter. Nobody has the Communion on his or her own. It is a meal we share with one another and our Host. It is the most marvelous meal in the world, and it nourishes us very deeply in our souls. That is why it is important to share in it regularly.

He offers us an audience. I happen to work for the archbishop of Canterbury. We have been friends for years. But welcoming though he is, it is very difficult to get in to see him these days. Appointments have to be made well in advance. He is simply too busy.

But God, amazingly, is not too busy to lend a listening ear to us. All through the Bible we are given invitations to cast our burdens on him, and he undertakes to carry them. We are bidden to ask and we will receive, to seek and we will find, to knock and it will be opened to us. A lovely bit in one of the psalms goes like this. God is seen as inviting us to meet with him: "Seek my face." And the psalmist responded, "Your face, Lord, I will seek." I find it very wonderful that God should give to you and me this unrestricted access into his presence. He is never too busy for us. He is never fed up with seeing us. And the enemy hates it. He knows full well that prayer is the source of spiritual power.

If the president offered to meet with you, I bet you would be there, bright-eyed and bushy-tailed, thrilled to bits with the privilege. Well, the King of kings invites us to have an audience with him, and not once in a lifetime, but on a regular basis. Three of the most remarkable words in the whole Bible are "pray without ceasing." This does not mean that we are to be praying all day long: that would be impossible. But surely it does mean that we can pray at any time, and that we are to avail ourselves of that privilege constantly.

Many people find books of prayers a help, or verses of hymns to be read and mulled over. Particularly when we are feeling low, it is a help to have this framework provided for us by other Christians. But the Lord also wants us to talk to him for ourselves from our hearts. He wants to hear us pour out our sorrows and joys into his listening ear. He wants to live with us, no less. People who live together talk together, do they not? It is meant to be like that with God. And if we persist in sharing our happiness, our requests, our thanksgivings, our confessions with him, we will grow. Indeed, we will grow so much that we begin to recognize his voice above the other voices that clamor for attention in our heads.

Listening to God, meditating before him, contemplating his beauty and holiness—these are some of the higher reaches of spirituality into which he will lead us as we are faithful in prayer. And increasingly we shall find that we love him not because of the good things he gives us; we shall love him for himself. But it is so easy to let prayer slip or give in to the subtle temptation that it really doesn't do much good—so why bother? Here again, we have a choice.

He offers us a community. It has been well said that the Christianity that does not begin with the individual does not begin; but the Christianity that ends with the individual ends. Following Jesus is a community business, not a solo trip from the alone to the Alone. To use one of the Bible's favorite images, we are like children adopted into a family. We need—and are not at liberty to choose—our brothers and sisters. Sometimes the New Testament sees us as branches in a great tree, or bricks in a building, or soldiers in an army, or limbs in a body. These pictures are always plural. You see, we are called into a new community. This is very important because it slays a couple of common misconceptions.

One is that I am the macho type who can soldier on by myself. I have my own ideas about God, and I do not need anything from you, thank you. That attitude is profoundly unchristian. We are not meant to be rugged individuals who fondly imagine we are independent. God tells us we can't cope adequately as Christians on our own, and we are not meant to try. We need one another. To fancy that we do not is to give way to an arrogance that stinks in God's nostrils.

The other misconception is that Christianity is all about saving souls. The New Testament rarely, if ever, uses this language. It is all about the kingdom of God, the community that is trying to make God King in every aspect of daily life, individual and corporate alike.

To be sure, the Lord wants to take us in hand and save us, to rescue us from the mess we have gotten ourselves into and to clean us up. He means to give us a fresh start, with him in control. But he wants to do a lot more than that. He wants to bring into being an alternative society to the selfish rat race that marks most of the Western world. He wants to cultivate in us not independence but interdependence. He wants us to be the rainbow people, of all shades and backgrounds, who reflect his sunlight against a dark and rainy background. He wants us to be a compassionate people in a hard world. He wants us to show that it is possible, and infinitely attractive, to live an upright, unselfish, generous life, marked by love for God and neighbor. This is not something any of us can do on our own. We need one another.

I reckon we need this togetherness at three levels. They were all a part of Judaism and passed over into Christianity. First is the small group of friends, meeting in a home. Second is the weekly synagogue or church meeting for worship and instruction. Third is the big celebration such as they had in the festivals at Jerusalem when sometimes a million and more would gather.

On the whole, the modern church is reasonably good on the synagogue form of meeting in a formal way on a Sunday morning. But it is weak on both the others. Many churches have no home fellowships whatsoever, and they are distinctly allergic to getting together in a large celebration with lots of other churches. In recent years, however, home groups have been multiplying at a tremendous rate, and they provide a natural forum for friendship, food, prayer, and sharing of the ordinary joys and sorrows of life with fellow Christians. They also form a splendid size for any practical task force to serve the community.

As for big gatherings, it is a thrill to worship with thousands of people in a convention in India or to be part of a great missions gathering like Urbana. I was moved recently to share in the March for Jesus in London, and look out over some seventy thousand people inundating Hyde Park and reveling in praise and prayer, song and dance, and joyful witness. Occasions like these remind us of what a big family we belong to across the globe and down the centuries. And we need that, especially if our local church is small and there are few other Christians in our workplace.

I believe we need all three levels of Christian fellowship so that we can genuinely be woven together into a lovely tapestry for God. In addition, many have found the need for one regular prayer partner or special spiritual friend with whom it is possible to share the deepest things. We have to choose how much Christian fellowship we will go for and what form it will take. God gives us perfect freedom to choose. It is an important decision, for fellowship is a vital means of growth.

CHOOSE TO BE OF SOME USE TO GOD

There is another significant area of choice that opens up more and more as the years go by. Whom are we going to live for? What is to be our guiding star? Ambition? Power? Money? A comfortable life? Sometimes these are burning passions; sometimes we slide into them without even realizing. But life is short, and we need to make up our minds on such a crucial issue.

I want to end this book with a plea. A plea that we take seriously the extent of the Lord's sacrifice for us and in return offer him the whole of our lives. A plea to allow him to direct us into paths he knows to be the best for us and for his kingdom. He has given us particular talents and endowments. Then let us choose to employ them in some way that furthers his principles of love and service to others, as befits citizens of the kingdom of heaven. It has very little to do with the actual occupations and careers we busy ourselves with. It has almost everything to do with our attitude and the way we conduct ourselves in daily life.

There is a marvelous passage about the lifestyle and impact of the early Christians in chapters five and six of an ancient book, the *Epistle to Diognetus,* which was written in the second century A.D. as the gospel began to make real inroads into secular society.

The distinction between Christians and other men does not lie in country or language or customs. . . . They follow local customs in clothing, food, and in the rest of life; and yet they exhibit the wonderfully paradoxical nature of their own citizenship. They live in their own countries, but as if they were resident aliens. They share all things as citizens and yet endure all things as if they were an underclass. Every foreign country is their homeland and every homeland a foreign country. They marry like everyone else, and have children: but they do not abort their young. They keep a common table but not a common bed. They live in the world but not in a worldly way. They enjoy a full life on earth, but their citizenship is in heaven. They obey the appointed laws, but they surpass the laws in their own lifestyle. They love everyone—and are universally derided. They are unknown—and roundly criticized. They are put to death—and gain life. They are poor but make many rich. They lack all things and yet have all things in abundance. They are dishonored and are glorified in their dishonor. . . . They are abused and they call down blessings in return. When they do good they are beaten up as ne'er-do-wells: when they are beaten up they rejoice as men who are given a new life. . . . In short, what the soul is in the body, that the Christians are in the world. The soul lives in the body but is not confined by the body, and the Christians live in the world but are not confined by the world. . . . God has appointed them to this great calling, and it would be wrong for them to decline it.

That description may be a bit idealized. It may be eighteen hundred years old. But isn't it a marvelous vision of what we Christians could be? Not just by the jobs we do and the way we do them, but by the kind of people we are. Those early Christians could not have given such a flavor to society had they not made the most vigorous and costly choice—to put Christ first in every aspect of their lives. They would certainly have agreed with the logic of C. T. Studd, a nineteenth-century international sportsman who gave up everything and went as a missionary to three continents—with incalculable consequences for good. He said, "If Jesus Christ is God and died for me, no sacrifice can be too great for me to make for him." We could do with more Christians of that caliber today, more who are prepared to face up to critical choices. We can't beat them, so let's join them.